MATH

LIVING
EDUCATION
■ level k

Angela O'Dell
& Carrie Bailey

MASTERBOOKS® CURRICULUM

Author: Angela O'Dell and Carrie Bailey

Master Books Creative Team:

Editor: Craig Froman

Design: Terry White

Cover Design: Diana Bogardus

Copy Editors: Judy Lewis

Curriculum Review:
Kristen Pratt
Laura Welch
Diana Bogardus

First printing: September 2019
Third printing: August 2020

Master Books® is a division of the New Leaf Publishing Group, Inc.

ISBN: 978-1-68344-176-2
ISBN: 978-1-61458-725-5 (digital)

All images are from shutterstock.com or istockphotos.com except page 248 by Diana Bogardus and page 364 by Carrie Bailey.

Unless otherwise noted, Scripture quotations are from the New King James Version of the Bible.

Printed in the United States of America

Please visit our website for other great titles:

www.masterbooks.com

Author Bios:

Angela O'Dell is a homeschooling mom and author who embraces many aspects of the Charlotte Mason method yet knows that modern children need an education that teaches clearly the never-changing truth of God and His Word. With this in mind, she has worked to bring a curriculum that reaches deep into the heart of children and their families. She has written over 20 books, including her history series and her math series.

Carrie Bailey is a Christian homeschool mom to three boys. She has a degree in early childhood education, and has also taught students with special needs in the public school system. She and her husband, Jesse, work in their home church serving in many capacities from media to curriculum decisions.

Scope and Sequence

Using This Course

Features: The suggested weekly schedule enclosed has easy-to-manage lessons that guide the reading, worksheets, and all assessments. The pages of this course are perforated and three-hole punched so materials are easy to tear out, hand out, grade, and store. Teachers are encouraged to adjust the schedule and materials needed in order to best work within their unique educational program.

Welcome to *Math Lessons for a Living Education*: The secular worldview has drilled into our heads and hearts that we as parents do not have what it takes to teach our children. This series has consistently demonstrated that God is more than able to help us guide our children into the truth. Now another resource in this series can help you through your child's formative years: *Math Lessons for a Living Education Teaching Companion*. It was created for the teacher to assist in math grades K through 6.

🕐	Approximately 30 minutes per lesson, five days a week, for 36 weeks
🔑	Puzzle answer keys are provided in the back
📑	Worksheets are included for each section
📄	Designed for grade K in a one-year course

Course Description

This book was written to be used by you and your young student together. It is the story of a twin brother and sister as they interact with their family, friends, and town. They begin making connections in life and find it is full of learning opportunities! As you read their story, your student will begin to feel a part of the twins' lives. They will learn about counting, basic shapes, opposites, positional words, graphing, and more. They will also learn about the weather, nature, and how unique God created them to be. They will be excited to join the twins as they encounter living math adventures. I hope you have a grand time on this adventure with the twins.

- ✔ Learn to count to 10 and numbers 0–10.
- ✔ Understand one-to-one correspondence up to 10.
- ✔ Explore weight and measurement through play and cooking.
- ✔ Make connections to their world by noticing basic patterns, shapes, and concepts of time.

How can mathematics be taught as a living subject?

Have you ever noticed that we tend to compartmentalize when teaching our children? In real life, there aren't artificial barriers between "subjects." For example, when you are cooking or baking, you have to use the skills of reading, logical thinking, and measuring, just to name a few. In driving a car, you see and read road signs, read maps, and count miles. So why do we say to our students, "This is math, this is language, this is science/nature, this is history. . . ?"

I have learned that it is most natural and most effective to teach children, not subjects. For example, one conversation, which was originally about telling time, turned into a story about when I was a child and completely burned a batch of cookies because I didn't set a timer. Out came the timer, which was scrutinized closely by all within hearing. Out came the cookbook, which was carefully perused by two sisters, who decide they would like to make cookies and remember to set the timer. Little sister asked if she could help by measuring, and Mom said, "You know, guys, while you are making the cookies, I will play the audio book CD that we started last night!"

In this story, what if I had said, "NO, we are sticking to telling time, and we are going to drill about how to learn to tell time!" A wonderful chance to bring math to life would have slipped by. Even more sadly, the children would not have the chance to actually use the skill. They would have missed the opportunity to see how telling time is only part of the picture — they would have missed out on why telling time is important for them to learn, and how it can help them in everyday life.

I am not saying that there aren't times to stick to the topic on hand, and I most certainly am not saying that there isn't a time and place for drill. But drill cannot take the place of math in real life. One without the other is like love without discipline or discipline without love. We have to have balance! It has become quite clear to me that there is an abundance of math programs available that are nothing but monotonous drill sheets dressed up in pretty colors. Pretty colors do not make a living book. Content, story, and the ability to show math in real life make a living math book.

Materials list for each lesson

It is suggested that certain items be made available to students each day. These would include something to write with (pencil or pen) and something to color with (crayons, colored pencils, or markers).

The following materials are recommended for specific lessons:

Lesson 1
- ☐ A board game that uses color recognition and number recognition

Lesson 2
- ☐ Small amount of paint to make fingerprints
- ☐ Items of various colors to play "I Spy"
- ☐ A board game that uses color recognition and number recognition

Lesson 3
- ☐ Objects around the house to sort by color (blocks or cards)
- ☐ Painter's tape or sidewalk chalk
- ☐ Cardstock (laminated if possible)
- ☐ Hole punch
- ☐ Shoe string

Lesson 4
- ☐ Paper clips
- ☐ Dirt, sidewalk chalk, gravel, or leaves (if outside)
- ☐ Cereal or beans (if inside)
- ☐ Items around the house that are square shaped
- ☐ Blocks, paper clips, or other "counters" for measuring

Lesson 5
- ☐ Objects or toys for tall/short, big/small comparisons

Lesson 6
- ☐ Painter's tape and post-it notes
- ☐ Toothpicks

Lesson 7
- ☐ No additional items needed

Lesson 8
- ☐ No additional items needed

Lesson 9
- ☐ Raisins, nuts, and/or dried fruit for measuring

- ☐ ¼ cup, ½ cup, and 1 cup measuring cups
- ☐ Three kinds of apples for tasting (other fruit can be substituted)
- ☐ Post-it notes
- ☐ Toothpicks or pencils
- ☐ Recipe includes: 2 granny smith apples, ½ stick butter, 1 cup sugar, 2 packages crescent rolls, 12 oz soda, 9 x 13 cake pan
- ☐ Water for measuring

Lesson 10
- ☐ Colored toothpicks with dispenser
- ☐ Measuring cups of various sizes
- ☐ Teaspoon
- ☐ Tablespoon
- ☐ Rice or cereal to measure
- ☐ Recipe includes: 1 ½ cup unsalted butter, ¾ cup powdered sugar, ¾ teaspoon salt, 1 ½ cup ground or finely chopped pecans, 4 ½ teaspoons vanilla, 3 cups flour

Lesson 11
- ☐ A toy
- ☐ Optional: items to put away using position words (in, on, below, etc.)

Lesson 12
- ☐ Small objects for jumping over

Lesson 13
- ☐ Dominoes
- ☐ Scissors

Lesson 14
- ☐ Measuring utensils for liquids and solids (including 1 tablespoon, 1 cup, and 1 quart)
- ☐ Flour or salt
- ☐ Recipe includes: 1 can each of black beans, red kidney beans, pinto beans, corn, as well as 1 lb. ground beef, 1 8 oz. can tomato sauce, and

taco seasoning (shredded cheddar cheese, sour cream, tortilla chips, lettuce, and tomatoes)

- ☐ Blocks

Lesson 15

- ☐ Leaves or cardstock
- ☐ Plain white paper
- ☐ Tape

Lesson 16

- ☐ A nickel, dime, and quarter
- ☐ Piece of plain white paper

Lesson 17

- ☐ Blocks

Lesson 18

- ☐ Blocks
- ☐ A die
- ☐ Dominoes

Lesson 19

- ☐ Post-it notes or index cards
- ☐ Painter's tape or sidewalk chalk

Lesson 20

- ☐ Blocks
- ☐ A die

Lesson 21

- ☐ No additional items needed

Lesson 22

- ☐ Jump rope
- ☐ Blocks

Lesson 23

- ☐ Post-it notes

Lesson 24

- ☐ Thread
- ☐ Globe or ball

Lesson 25

- ☐ No additional items needed

Lesson 26

- ☐ Blocks
- ☐ A die

Lesson 27

- ☐ No additional items needed

Lesson 28

- ☐ Small toys or items from nature
- ☐ Sidewalk chalk for number line
- ☐ Pot/pan
- ☐ Wooden spoon

Lesson 29

- ☐ Hula hoops
- ☐ Blue toys (or books)
- ☐ Red toys (or books)
- ☐ Blue and red toys (or books)

Lesson 30

- ☐ Craft sticks
- ☐ Glue
- ☐ Tissue paper
- ☐ Scissors
- ☐ String or yarn

Lesson 31

- ☐ No additional items needed

Lesson 32

- ☐ 10 blocks or other counters
- ☐ Book
- ☐ Table

Lesson 33

- ☐ Bathroom scale
- ☐ Ball
- ☐ Clear glass jars
- ☐ Post-it notes
- ☐ Buttons or other counters

Lesson 34

- ☐ Items for pretend store (toys, etc.)
- ☐ Pennies, nickels, dimes, and quarters

Lesson 35

- ☐ 2 pieces of paper
- ☐ Marker to write on paper

Lesson 36

- ☐ No additional items needed

Calendar Concepts

Each weekly lesson has a prompt for completing an optional calendar activity. The two-sided calendar page is in the back of the book, and can be removed and laminated for ease of use. Using an erasable marker, you can fill in the calendar each day and talk with your students about days, weeks, weekends, and months as you move through the math pages. Each daily exercise has several prompts to go over.

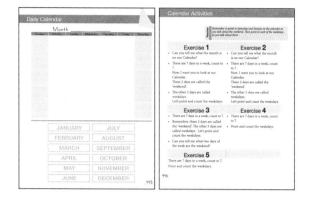

Grading subjective assignments

Most often with math the grading is very objective. For example, 2 + 2 = 4, and no amount of individual expression changes this answer. However, there are times in this course when the answer may depend on a student's reflections of what he or she has learned on a particular day or in a week of assignments. In these subjective cases, the teacher can base a grade for these responses on several more objective measures. Does the student seem to understand the question and answer it as clearly as possible? Does the answer seem complete or does it fail to answer all aspects of the question? So a student may receive full credit if they seemed to meet all the assignment requirements, may get a passing grade if they meet some of the requirements, or may need to repeat the assignment if they didn't meet any of the requirements.

A – Student showed complete mastery of concepts with no errors.

B – Student showed mastery of concepts with minimal errors.

C – Student showed partial mastery of concepts. Review of some concepts is needed.

D – Student showed minimal understanding of concepts. Review is needed.

F – Student did not show understanding of concepts. Review is needed.

First Semester Suggested Daily Schedule

Date	Day	Assignment	Due Date	✓	Grade
		First Semester-First Quarter			
Week 1	Day 1	Read Lesson 1 • Pages 15–16 Complete Lesson 1 Exercise 1 • Pages 17–18			
	Day 2	Complete Lesson 1 Exercise 2 • Pages 19–20			
	Day 3	Complete Lesson 1 Exercise 3 • Pages 21–22			
	Day 4	Complete Lesson 1 Exercise 4 • Page 23			
	Day 5	Complete Lesson 1 Exercise 5 • Page 24			
Week 2	Day 6	Read Lesson 2 • Pages 25–26 Complete Lesson 2 Exercise 1 • Page 27			
	Day 7	Complete Lesson 2 Exercise 2 • Page 28			
	Day 8	Complete Lesson 2 Exercise 3 • Pages 29–30			
	Day 9	Complete Lesson 2 Exercise 4 • Pages 31–32			
	Day 10	Complete Lesson 2 Exercise 5 • Pages 33–34			
Week 3	Day 11	Read Lesson 3 • Pages 35–36 Complete Lesson 3 Exercise 1 • Page 37			
	Day 12	Complete Lesson 3 Exercise 2 • Pages 38–39			
	Day 13	Complete Lesson 3 Exercise 3 • Page 40			
	Day 14	Complete Lesson 3 Exercise 4 • Page 41			
	Day 15	Complete Lesson 3 Exercise 5 • Page 42			
Week 4	Day 16	Read Lesson 4 • Pages 43–44 Complete Lesson 4 Exercise 1 • Pages 45–46			
	Day 17	Complete Lesson 4 Exercise 2 • Pages 47–48			
	Day 18	Complete Lesson 4 Exercise 3 • Pages 49–50			
	Day 19	Complete Lesson 4 Exercise 4 • Pages 51–52			
	Day 20	Complete Lesson 4 Exercise 5 • Pages 53–54			
Week 5	Day 21	Read Lesson 5 • Pages 55–56 Complete Lesson 5 Exercise 1 • Pages 57–58			
	Day 22	Complete Lesson 5 Exercise 2 • Pages 59–60			
	Day 23	Complete Lesson 5 Exercise 3 • Pages 61–62			
	Day 24	Complete Lesson 5 Exercise 4 • Pages 63–64			
	Day 25	Complete Lesson 5 Exercise 5 • Pages 65–66			
Week 6	Day 26	Read Lesson 6 • Pages 67–68 Complete Lesson 6 Exercise 1 • Pages 69–70			
	Day 27	Complete Lesson 6 Exercise 2 • Pages 71–72			
	Day 28	Complete Lesson 6 Exercise 3 • Pages 73–74			
	Day 29	Complete Lesson 6 Exercise 4 • Pages 75–76			
	Day 30	Complete Lesson 6 Exercise 5 • Pages 77–78			

Date	Day	Assignment	Due Date	✓	Grade
Week 7	Day 31	Read Lesson 7 • Pages 79–80 Complete Lesson 7 Exercise 1 • Pages 81–82			
	Day 32	Complete Lesson 7 Exercise 2 • Pages 83–84			
	Day 33	Complete Lesson 7 Exercise 3 • Pages 85–86			
	Day 34	Complete Lesson 7 Exercise 4 • Pages 87–88			
	Day 35	Complete Lesson 7 Exercise 5 • Pages 89–90			
Week 8	Day 36	Read Lesson 8 • Pages 91–92 Complete Lesson 8 Exercise 1 • Pages 93–94			
	Day 37	Complete Lesson 8 Exercise 2 • Pages 95–96			
	Day 38	Complete Lesson 8 Exercise 3 • Pages 97–98			
	Day 39	Complete Lesson 8 Exercise 4 • Pages 99–100			
	Day 40	Complete Lesson 8 Exercise 5 • Pages 101–102			
Week 9	Day 41	Read Lesson 9 • Pages 103–104 Complete Lesson 9 Exercise 1 • Pages 105–106			
	Day 42	Complete Lesson 9 Exercise 2 • Pages 107–108			
	Day 43	Complete Lesson 9 Exercise 3 • Pages 109–110			
	Day 44	Complete Lesson 9 Exercise 4 • Pages 111–112			
	Day 45	Complete Lesson 9 Exercise 5 • Pages 113–114			
First Semester-Second Quarter					
Week 1	Day 46	Read Lesson 10 • Pages 115–116 Complete Lesson 10 Exercise 1 • Pages 117–118			
	Day 47	Complete Lesson 10 Exercise 2 • Pages 119–120			
	Day 48	Complete Lesson 10 Exercise 3 • Pages 121–122			
	Day 49	Complete Lesson 10 Exercise 4 • Pages 123–124			
	Day 50	Complete Lesson 10 Exercise 5 • Pages 125–126			
Week 2	Day 51	Read Lesson 11 • Pages 127–128 Complete Lesson 11 Exercise 1 • Pages 129–130			
	Day 52	Complete Lesson 11 Exercise 2 • Pages 131–132			
	Day 53	Complete Lesson 11 Exercise 3 • Pages 133–134			
	Day 54	Complete Lesson 11 Exercise 4 • Pages 135–136			
	Day 55	Complete Lesson 11 Exercise 5 • Pages 137–138			
Week 3	Day 56	Read Lesson 12 • Pages 139–140 Complete Lesson 12 Exercise 1 • Pages 141–142			
	Day 57	Complete Lesson 12 Exercise 2 • Pages 143–144			
	Day 58	Complete Lesson 12 Exercise 3 • Pages 145–146			
	Day 59	Complete Lesson 12 Exercise 4 • Pages 147–148			
	Day 60	Complete Lesson 12 Exercise 5 • Pages 149–150			
Week 4	Day 61	Read Lesson 13 • Pages 151–152 Complete Lesson 13 Exercise 1 • Pages 153–154			
	Day 62	Complete Lesson 13 Exercise 2 • Pages 155–156			
	Day 63	Complete Lesson 13 Exercise 3 • Pages 157–158			
	Day 64	Complete Lesson 13 Exercise 4 • Pages 159–160			
	Day 65	Complete Lesson 13 Exercise 5 • Pages 161–162			

Date	Day	Assignment	Due Date	✓	Grade
Week 5	Day 66	Read Lesson 14 • Pages 163–164 Complete Lesson 14 Exercise 1 • Pages 165–166			
	Day 67	Complete Lesson 14 Exercise 2 • Pages 167–168			
	Day 68	Complete Lesson 14 Exercise 3 • Pages 169–170			
	Day 69	Complete Lesson 14 Exercise 4 • Pages 171–172			
	Day 70	Complete Lesson 14 Exercise 5 • Pages 173–174			
Week 6	Day 71	Read Lesson 15 • Pages 175–176 Complete Lesson 15 Exercise 1 • Pages 177–178			
	Day 72	Complete Lesson 15 Exercise 2 • Pages 179–180			
	Day 73	Complete Lesson 15 Exercise 3 • Pages 181–182			
	Day 74	Complete Lesson 15 Exercise 4 • Pages 183–184			
	Day 75	Complete Lesson 15 Exercise 5 • Pages 185–186			
Week 7	Day 76	Read Lesson 16 • Pages 187–188 Complete Lesson 16 Exercise 1 • Page 189–190			
	Day 77	Complete Lesson 16 Exercise 2 • Pages 191–192			
	Day 78	Complete Lesson 16 Exercise 3 • Pages 193–194			
	Day 79	Complete Lesson 16 Exercise 4 • Pages 195–196			
	Day 80	Complete Lesson 16 Exercise 5 • Pages 197–198			
Week 8	Day 81	Read Lesson 17 • Pages 199–200 Complete Lesson 17 Exercise 1 • Pages 201–202			
	Day 82	Complete Lesson 17 Exercise 2 • Pages 203–204			
	Day 83	Complete Lesson 17 Exercise 3 • Pages 205–206			
	Day 84	Complete Lesson 17 Exercise 4 • Pages 207–208			
	Day 85	Complete Lesson 17 Exercise 5 • Pages 209–210			
Week 9	Day 86	Read Lesson 18 • Pages 211–212 Complete Lesson 18 Exercise 1 • Pages 213–214			
	Day 87	Complete Lesson 18 Exercise 2 • Pages 215–216			
	Day 88	Complete Lesson 18 Exercise 3 • Pages 217–218			
	Day 89	Complete Lesson 18 Exercise 4 • Pages 219–220			
	Day 90	Complete Lesson 18 Exercise 5 • Pages 221–222			
		Mid-Term Grade			

Second Semester Suggested Daily Schedule

Date	Day	Assignment	Due Date	✓	Grade
		Second Semester-Third Quarter			
Week 1	Day 91	Read Lesson 19 • Pages 223–224 Complete Lesson 19 Exercise 1 • Pages 225–226			
	Day 92	Complete Lesson 19 Exercise 2 • Pages 227–228			
	Day 93	Complete Lesson 19 Exercise 3 • Pages 229–230			
	Day 94	Complete Lesson 19 Exercise 4 • Pages 231–232			
	Day 95	Complete Lesson 19 Exercise 5 • Pages 233–234			
Week 2	Day 96	Read Lesson 20 • Pages 235–236 Complete Lesson 20 Exercise 1 • Pages 237–238			
	Day 97	Complete Lesson 20 Exercise 2 • Pages 239–240			
	Day 98	Complete Lesson 20 Exercise 3 • Pages 241–242			
	Day 99	Complete Lesson 20 Exercise 4 • Pages 243–244			
	Day 100	Complete Lesson 20 Exercise 5 • Pages 245–246			
Week 3	Day 101	Read Lesson 21 • Pages 247–248 Complete Lesson 21 Exercise 1 • Pages 249–250			
	Day 102	Complete Lesson 21 Exercise 2 • Pages 251–252			
	Day 103	Complete Lesson 21 Exercise 3 • Pages 253–254			
	Day 104	Complete Lesson 21 Exercise 4 • Pages 255–256			
	Day 105	Complete Lesson 21 Exercise 5 • Pages 257–258			
Week 4	Day 106	Read Lesson 22 • Pages 259–260 Complete Lesson 22 Exercise 1 • Pages 261–262			
	Day 107	Complete Lesson 22 Exercise 2 • Pages 263–264			
	Day 108	Complete Lesson 22 Exercise 3 • Pages 265–266			
	Day 109	Complete Lesson 22 Exercise 4 • Pages 267–268			
	Day 110	Complete Lesson 22 Exercise 5 • Pages 269–270			
Week 5	Day 111	Read Lesson 23 • Pages 271–272 Complete Lesson 23 Exercise 1 • Pages 273–274			
	Day 112	Complete Lesson 23 Exercise 2 • Pages 275–276			
	Day 113	Complete Lesson 23 Exercise 3 • Pages 277–278			
	Day 114	Complete Lesson 23 Exercise 4 • Pages 279–280			
	Day 115	Complete Lesson 23 Exercise 5 • Pages 281–282			
Week 6	Day 116	Read Lesson 24 • Pages 283–284 Complete Lesson 24 Exercise 1 • Pages 285–286			
	Day 117	Complete Lesson 24 Exercise 2 • Pages 287–288			
	Day 118	Complete Lesson 24 Exercise 3 • Pages 289–290			
	Day 119	Complete Lesson 24 Exercise 4 • Pages 291–292			
	Day 120	Complete Lesson 24 Exercise 5 • Pages 293–294			

Math Level K

Date	Day	Assignment	Due Date	✓	Grade
Week 7	Day 121	Read Lesson 25 • Pages 295–296 Complete Lesson 25 Exercise 1 • Pages 297–298			
	Day 122	Complete Lesson 25 Exercise 2 • Pages 299–300			
	Day 123	Complete Lesson 25 Exercise 3 • Pages 301–302			
	Day 124	Complete Lesson 25 Exercise 4 • Pages 303–304			
	Day 125	Complete Lesson 25 Exercise 5 • Pages 305–306			
Week 8	Day 126	Read Lesson 26 • Pages 307–308 Complete Lesson 26 Exercise 1 • Pages 309–310			
	Day 127	Complete Lesson 26 Exercise 2 • Pages 311–312			
	Day 128	Complete Lesson 26 Exercise 3 • Pages 313–314			
	Day 129	Complete Lesson 26 Exercise 4 • Pages 315–316			
	Day 130	Complete Lesson 26 Exercise 5 • Pages 317–318			
Week 9	Day 131	Read Lesson 27 • Pages 319–320 Complete Lesson 27 Exercise 1 • Pages 321–322			
	Day 132	Complete Lesson 27 Exercise 2 • Pages 323–324			
	Day 133	Complete Lesson 27 Exercise 3 • Pages 325–326			
	Day 134	Complete Lesson 27 Exercise 4 • Pages 327–328			
	Day 135	Complete Lesson 27 Exercise 5 • Pages 329–330			
Second Semester-Fourth Quarter					
Week 1	Day 136	Read Lesson 28 • Pages 331–332 Complete Lesson 28 Exercise 1 • Pages 333–334			
	Day 137	Complete Lesson 28 Exercise 2 • Pages 335–336			
	Day 138	Complete Lesson 28 Exercise 3 • Pages 337–338			
	Day 139	Complete Lesson 28 Exercise 4 • Pages 339–340			
	Day 140	Complete Lesson 28 Exercise 5 • Pages 341–342			
Week 2	Day 141	Read Lesson 29 • Pages 343–344 Complete Lesson 29 Exercise 1 • Pages 345–346			
	Day 142	Complete Lesson 29 Exercise 2 • Pages 347–348			
	Day 143	Complete Lesson 29 Exercise 3 • Pages 349–350			
	Day 144	Complete Lesson 29 Exercise 4 • Pages 351–352			
	Day 145	Complete Lesson 29 Exercise 5 • Pages 353–354			
Week 3	Day 146	Read Lesson 30 • Pages 355–356 Complete Lesson 30 Exercise 1 • Pages 357–358			
	Day 147	Complete Lesson 30 Exercise 2 • Pages 359–360			
	Day 148	Complete Lesson 30 Exercise 3 • Pages 361–362			
	Day 149	Complete Lesson 30 Exercise 4 • Pages 363–364			
	Day 150	Complete Lesson 30 Exercise 5 • Pages 365–366			
Week 4	Day 151	Read Lesson 31 • Pages 367–368 Complete Lesson 31 Exercise 1• Pages 369–370			
	Day 152	Complete Lesson 31 Exercise 2 • Pages 371–372			
	Day 153	Complete Lesson 31 Exercise 3 • Pages 373–374			
	Day 154	Complete Lesson 31 Exercise 4 • Pages 375–376			
	Day 155	Complete Lesson 31 Exercise 5 • Pages 377–378			

Date	Day	Assignment	Due Date	✓	Grade
Week 5	Day 156	Read Lesson 32 • Pages 379–380 Complete Lesson 32 Exercise 1 • Pages 381–382			
	Day 157	Complete Lesson 32 Exercise 2 • Pages 383–384			
	Day 158	Complete Lesson 32 Exercise 3 • Pages 385–386			
	Day 159	Complete Lesson 32 Exercise 4 • Pages 387–388			
	Day 160	Complete Lesson 32 Exercise 5 • Pages 389–390			
Week 6	Day 161	Read Lesson 33 • Pages 391–392 Complete Lesson 33 Exercise 1 • Pages 393–394			
	Day 162	Complete Lesson 33 Exercise 2 • Pages 395–396			
	Day 163	Complete Lesson 33 Exercise 3 • Pages 397–398			
	Day 164	Complete Lesson 33 Exercise 4 • Pages 399–400			
	Day 165	Complete Lesson 33 Exercise 5 • Pages 401–402			
Week 7	Day 166	Read Lesson 34 • Pages 403–404 Complete Lesson 34 Exercise 1 • Pages 405–406			
	Day 167	Complete Lesson 34 Exercise 2 • Pages 407–408			
	Day 168	Complete Lesson 34 Exercise 3 • Pages 409–410			
	Day 169	Complete Lesson 34 Exercise 4 • Pages 411–412			
	Day 170	Complete Lesson 34 Exercise 5 • Pages 413–414			
Week 8	Day 171	Read Lesson 35 • Pages 415–416 Complete Lesson 35 Exercise 1 • Pages 417–418			
	Day 172	Complete Lesson 35 Exercise 2 • Pages 419–420			
	Day 173	Complete Lesson 35 Exercise 3 • Pages 421–422			
	Day 174	Complete Lesson 35 Exercise 4 • Pages 423–424			
	Day 175	Complete Lesson 35 Exercise 5 • Pages 425–426			
Week 9	Day 176	Read Lesson 36 • Pages 427–428 Complete Lesson 36 Exercise 1 • Pages 429–432			
	Day 177	Complete Lesson 36 Exercise 2 • Pages 433–436			
	Day 178	Complete Lesson 36 Exercise 3 • Pages 437–438			
	Day 179	Complete Lesson 36 Exercise 4 • Pages 439–440			
	Day 180	Complete Lesson 36 Exercise 5 • Pages 441–442			
		Final Grade			

Counting to 5, Circles, and Calendar Concepts

"Mama, when is it going to stop raining?" Charlie's question was muffled because his nose was pressed against the living room window. It seemed like it had been raining forever! Charlie's twin sister, Charlotte, stood next to him and stared out at the gray sky. It was the middle of April, and the cold, Minnesota winter had given way to a warm but soggy, wet spring. The twins' mom came to stand behind her two unhappy children. She wished it would stop raining, too.

"Children, why don't you come into the kitchen with me?" she asked as she placed a hand on each of their heads. Sighing, they both nodded and turned away from the window.

"Can we help you make cookies, Mama?" Charlotte asked hopefully.

"Sure! Why don't we make Daddy his favorite molasses cookies?" Mama was happy to see the children smile. As the rain continued to pitter-patter on the kitchen window awning, the three of them sang songs and worked together to stir up a batch of special cookies for Daddy.

They were having such a grand time together, they did not even realize that the rain had stopped until the sun was shining brightly through the window and into the kitchen.

"Mama! It stopped raining!" Charlie shouted. He had run back to his place at the living room window. "Wow!" he exclaimed in awe, "Look at the rainbow!" Charlotte raced to stand next to him, wiping her floury hands across her forehead to move the hair out of her eyes.

"Mama! Come look!" Charlotte called over her shoulder. "It's the brightest rainbow I've ever seen before! Can we go outside to play now? Please?" Charlotte turned her face up to her mom.

"Yes, I don't see why not!" her mom answered as she wiped Charlotte's forehead with the corner of her apron. "Make sure you both put on your rubber boots!" she called out after her children, who had raced to the coat closet by the back door.

"Wooohooo! I love spring!" Charlie hooted in glee.

"Come on, Charlie, let's go outside to see the rainbow!" Charlotte urged her brother.

Calendar:

☐ Complete the calendar.
☐ Review on back of calendar.

Teacher

See front matter for instruction on how to teach calendar concepts.

These concepts are taught over the whole year. They are not going to grasp this all yet, but it is a simple basic introduction.

Application:

Have you ever seen a rainbow? I bet when you have seen a rainbow that you thought it was only part of a circle like this.

A rainbow is actually a full circle! You can only see part of it unless you are up in the sky at a certain angle. A rainbow stands for a promise from God.

Notice that a circle has no stopping points. It is kind of like a ball. Look around and see if you can find things that are shaped like a circle.

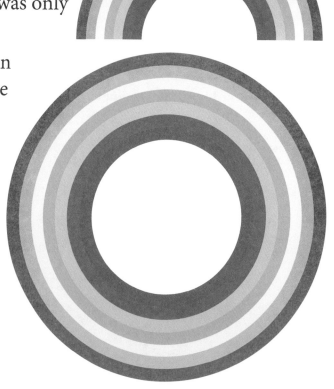

Critical Thinking:

Let's learn about different kinds of lines. Trace them with your finger.

This is a straight line. Count the straight line. One!

This is a curved line. Count the straight line and the curved line. One, two!

This line is both curved and straight.
Count all the lines. One, two, three!

Which number below is blue with a curved line?

Which one is orange with a straight line?

1 2 3 4

- Circle the ball that is purple.
- Put a mark on the ball that is red.
- Count all the balls. One, two, three, four!

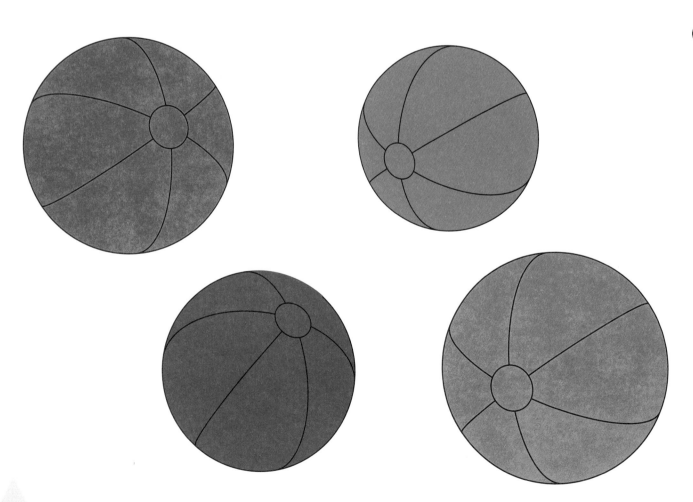

Application:

- Trace the circles on the page with your finger.
- How many circles do you have?

Now, count to 5.
One, two, three, four, five!

Teacher
If a student struggles to count on his or her own, just repeat this throughout the day, even sing a rhyme with it. They do not need to count items, just count.

Critical Thinking:

Can you find me? Point to the right answer.

- I am wearing a red dress.
- I have a blue apron on.
- I have a red bow and blue shoes.
- I am wearing a green apron.

Now, count all the smiles. One, two, three, four!

Application:

Counting objects is fun! When we count items, we often touch them as we count.

Look at the picture of the cupboard and count all five items. Point to each item as you count.

One, two, three, four, five!

Let's do it again and hop as we count.

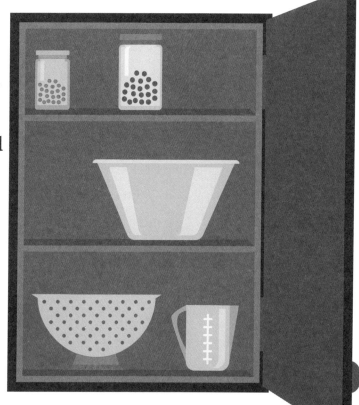

Critical Thinking:

- Circle the red shape.
- Do you know what shape it is?

- Use a blue crayon to draw a line to connect the blue shapes.
- Use a red crayon to connect the red shapes.
- Use a green crayon to connect the green shapes.

Application:

Let's play a game!

Critical Thinking:

Can you find me?

- How many kids have a white shirt? (One!)
- How many kids have stripes on their shirts? (Two!)
- How many kids have blue pants or shorts? (Three!)
- How many girls are there? (Four!)
- How many kids are standing up? (Five!)

Teacher *Play a board game using color recognition and number recognition, such as Chutes & Ladders® or Candy Land®, etc.*

Do you know about the four seasons? There is fall, winter, spring, and summer. Fall or autumn is generally when the world gets cooler and leaves start to fall off the trees. Then comes winter, generally the coldest time of the year when it sometimes snows. After that the spring comes, when flowers and plants grow again, and it gets warmer. Finally, there is summer, the hottest time of the year. Say them with me now: fall, winter, spring, and summer!

Do you remember what season Charlie and Charlotte were in as their story started? It was spring!

Four Seasons

Application:

Trace and count the circles. One, two, three, four, five!

Critical Thinking:

Complete the picture by copying.

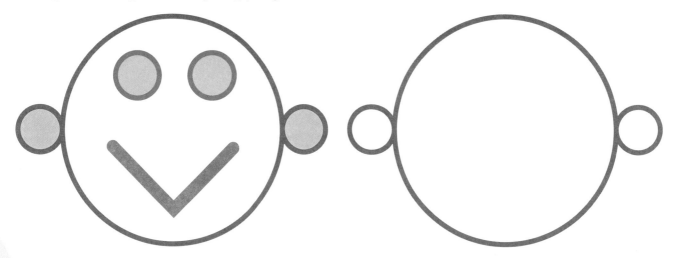

Counting to 5, Ovals, and Seasons

"Children, make sure you put on the sweatshirts I laid on your beds." Mom poked her head in the door of the twins' bedroom. "It might be spring now, but it is still cool outside."

"Yes, Mama," Charlotte replied as she wiggled her toes down into her socks. Putting on socks could be very challenging! Sometimes, as hard as she tried, Charlotte still ended up with the heel of her sock sticking out on the top of her foot. She smiled. Today, her socks had gone on correctly on the first try!

"I sure am glad I don't have to wear my big, heavy winter boots anymore," Charlie grinned as he stuffed his feet into his sneakers and jumped to his feet. Something wasn't right . . . he looked down at his feet. His shoes were on the wrong feet, again. Sighing, Charlie sat on the side of his bed to fix his shoes.

He was so excited! Grandma and Grandpa had come for a visit, and the whole family was going to the zoo for an outing. "Grandpa, aren't you glad we don't have to wear our winter coats now?" Charlie asked with a mouthful of pancakes. "Sorry, Mama," he swallowed before finishing his question. "And me and Charlotte . . . umm, Charlotte and I, we get to wear our new sweatshirts!" Charlie pulled his hood up to show his grandparents just how wonderful his new sweatshirt was.

"That's a nice sweatshirt, Charlie," Grandpa Peter said with a twinkle in his eye. "Did you know that the sheep on our farm had their winter coats taken off a couple of weeks ago?" The twins glanced at each other. Grandpa was known for his jokes. Was this one of them?

They both looked at Grandma to see if she was smiling. She was. "Grandpa is right, children," she said with a smile. "Our sheep went through their spring shearing two weeks ago." She went on to explain that sheep grow extremely thick, wooly winter coats during the cold months. These coats have to be removed in a process called shearing each spring. The wool is then sold to be made into cloth for coats, blankets, and other warm products.

"Do you think we will see any sheep at the zoo, Dad?" Charlotte asked. She certainly hoped so. She wanted to see sheep without their winter coats! She wondered if they had sweatshirts…

Calendar:

☐   Complete the calendar.
☐   Review on back of calendar.

Application:

An oval looks like this.

Ovals are like stretched-out circles.

Make a sheep using your thumbprints as the body, add a small oval for the head, and draw a face on it. Add lines for the legs, and a small tail.

Count to three together.

Teacher

Play a game of "I Spy" using colors. (I spy something that is: purple, red, and yellow.)

Critical Thinking:

Let's play a game!

I love the beautiful flowers of spring.
These three early flowers are purple, red, and yellow.

Application:

- Trace the ovals with your finger.
- Color one purple, one red, and one yellow.
- Count to three together. One, two, three.

Critical Thinking:

Let's play a game!

Teacher

Play a board game using color recognition and number recognition, such as Chutes & Ladders® or Candy Land®, etc.

Application:

- Trace the ovals and count them.
- Count by touching under each one.

Now, we will count to five together. One, two, three, four, five.

Clap as you count to five. Hop on one foot as you count to five (try to not hold on to anything or anyone). Hop on the other foot as you count to five.

Critical Thinking:

Match the pictures with the correct season. How many seasons are there? Four!

Math Level K – Lesson 2

Application:

Circle 5 objects in each box. Touch them as you count.

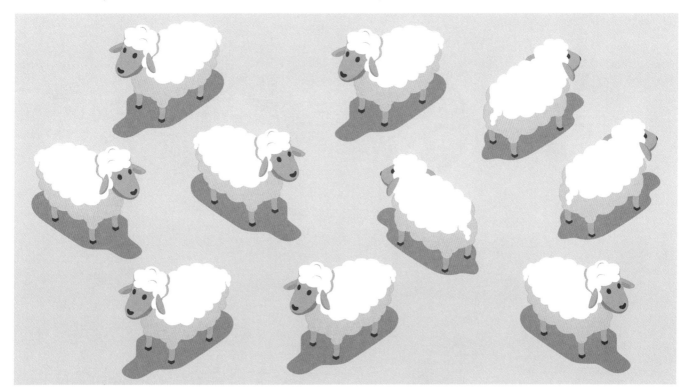

Critical Thinking:

Match the pictures with the correct season. Count the seasons. One, two, three, four.

Application:

Draw a person with an oval face, ears, and nose. Use any other lines or shapes for their body.

Critical Thinking:

What is your favorite season?

What is something about that season that you enjoy?

Color these spring flowers purple, red and yellow.

Counting to 7, Triangles, and Number Line

"Children, please make sure you keep the playdough on the table," Mom reminded Charlie and Charlotte as she washed dishes. It was raining outside, so the children were seated at the kitchen table, listening to an audiobook and playing with playdough.

"We will, Mama. Charlie, look at what I made," Charlotte said proudly. "I made a whole bunch of trees . . . like the ones by Grandma and Grandpa's farm. You know, the ones that never lose their leaves!"

Charlie nodded with a smile. "Those are really good trees, Charlotte," he said kindly. "What do you think of mine?"

"Umm. What is it?" Charlotte asked with a puzzled voice as she stared at Charlie's creation.

"It's a snake," Charlie grinned. "I like snakes." He made his dough snake "wiggle" across the table toward his sister. Charlotte shuddered. She didn't like snakes — even ones made from dough. "Now I'm gonna make something else. I'm gonna make some different shapes — like this," Charlie declared.

Charlotte watched as her brother used a plastic knife to cut up a clump of dough. He worked silently until he had created a strange, three-sided shape. "What's that called, Charlie?" Charlotte asked.

"I'm not sure what it's called," Charlie answered, "but I know I've seen this before. Mom, can you tell us what this shape is called?"

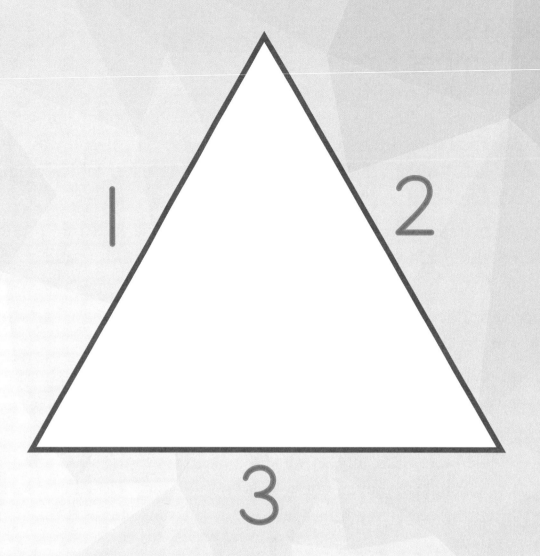

Their mom came over to the table and studied Charlie's dough shape. "That's a triangle, Charlie. See how it has three sides? All triangles have three sides," she explained to her children. "Good job, Charlie."

"I'm going to make triangles, too," Charlotte proclaimed. "I can make triangles for the top of my trees!" The children worked together to create a whole forest of triangle trees from their dough. Triangles were fun to create!

Calendar:

- ☐ Complete the calendar.
- ☐ Review on back of calendar.

Application:

Color the triangle-shaped trees.

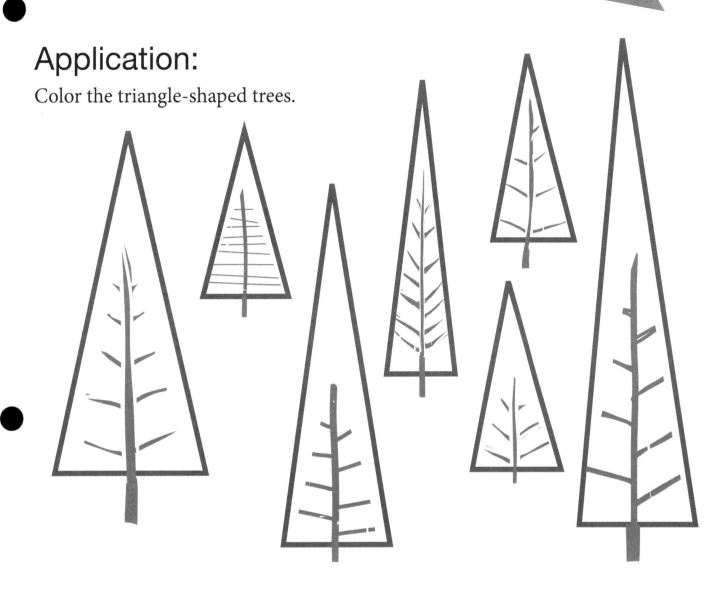

Now, we are going to count to seven together by touching each triangle tree one by one. One, two, three, four, five, six, seven.

Clap as you count to 7 this time. Now, stomp as you count to 7.

Critical Thinking:

Let's sort things by color!

Teacher

Using objects around the house, have them sort them by colors. These might include blocks or cards.

Let's draw a picture for each of the four seasons. Then count the items you have in each picture, like the number of flowers in spring or leaves in fall.

Spring

Summer

Fall

Winter

Application:

Start at 0 and hop like a bunny from 0–5 as you count to 5. Count aloud to 5. Clap as you count to 5.

Teacher
Use painter's tape or sidewalk chalk to make a number line of 0–5. (You will use this again this week.)

| 0 | 1 | 2 | 3 | 4 | 5 |

Critical Thinking:

Trace the following triangles with a pencil or crayon.

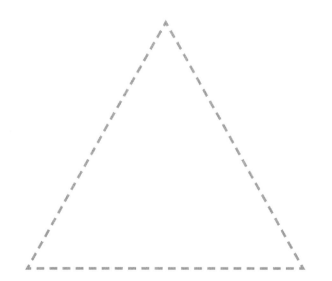
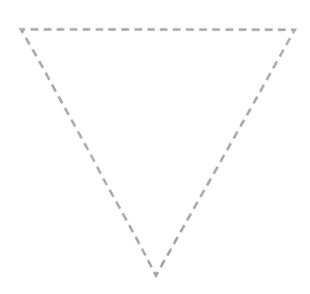

Application:

Trace the triangles.

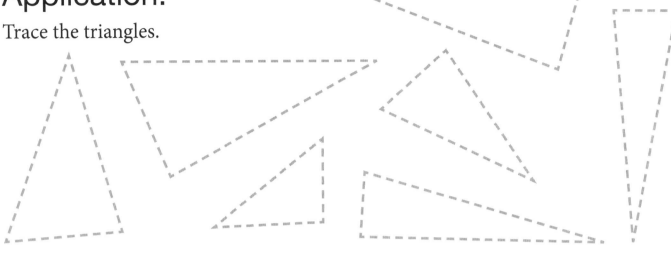

Count how many triangles there are.

Use your number line from yesterday and add two more so you can hop and count to 7 this time.

This time try hopping on one foot. Switch feet and do it again.

Critical Thinking:

Seasons Match: Match the person from each season with that season's picture.

Application:

Let's have some triangle fun!

Teacher

Cut triangles out of cardstock (laminate for more durability). Take a hole punch and punch holes approximately ½ inch apart on each side. Use a shoestring to have them lace the triangle.

Critical Thinking:

A triangle has 3 sides. A point is where two lines connect. How many points does the triangle have? Touch the points of the triangle.

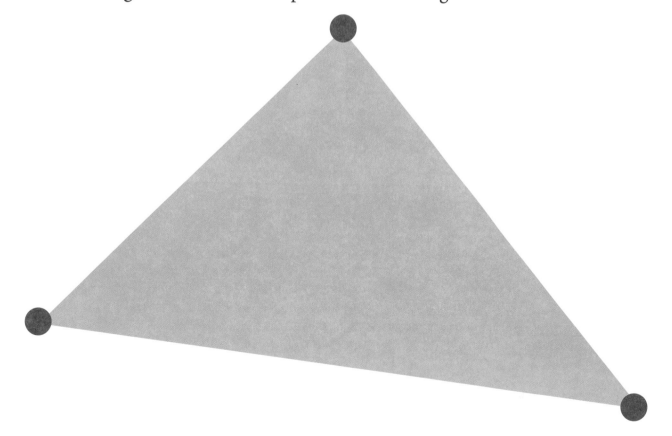

Application:

Draw a triangle below.

Critical Thinking:

Who am I?

1. I am tall with a long neck. Who am I?

2. I like to eat grass. I say moo. Who am I?

3. I slide around on my belly. Who am I?

Counting to 7, Squares, and Shape Matching

"One block, two blocks, three blocks, four blocks, aaaand . . . five blocks mmm mmm," hummed Charlotte as she carefully balanced the very last square, wooden block at the top of her block tower. She liked squares — they were easy to build with because all of their sides were the same length. "Charlie, look! See what I made?" she stood up, being extremely careful not to knock over her creation.

"Whoa! That's really tall, Charlotte! But you used some of my blocks too! That's not fair," Charlie scowled at his twin. "MOM! Charlotte took some of my blocks. Now I can't finish what I wanted to make," Charlie's frown had turned into an angry face. His foot began to draw back to kick the tower, and Charlotte let out a wail, "NOOO, Charlie! MOOOM! Charlie is going to kick over my tower!"

"What on earth!" Mom poked her head around the corner. "What are you two doing? Charlie put your foot down. You will not kick Charlotte's tower. That is unkind and is simply not the way we behave in this family. Use your words, not your feet or fists to settle a problem." Charlotte sighed. Her block tower had been saved.

"Charlotte," Mom continued, "you know better than to take what isn't yours. Your tower is nice, but you must give Charlie back his blocks. I think both of you need to put away your toys and come help me with some chores." The twins looked at each other and silently began putting away their blocks.

"Charlie, I would like you to match the socks in this basket. Charlotte, you may help me fold Daddy's t-shirts." The children nodded and quietly set to work. "Children, I want you to grow up to be kind and considerate people, and learning to control your anger is an important part of that. It is important to be kind now, so it will be part of your character when you are an adult. Folding Daddy's laundry for him is kind; he works hard to take care of us. Charlotte, watch as I show you how to fold his t-shirts. We need to be careful, so they are not wrinkled when he needs to wear them. First, you lay them out — nice and smooth like this. Then you fold each of the arms in like this. Last, fold the shirt into a square — like this."

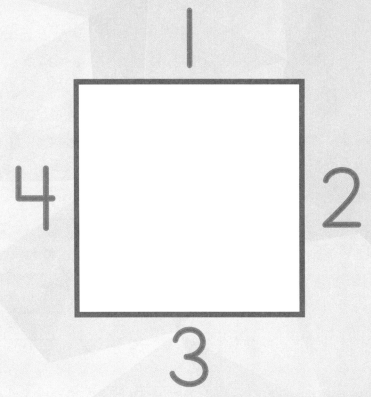

Charlotte nodded and went to work on another shirt. When it was finished, it was a square. She stacked it on top of the other shirts. She liked squares. They had four sides that were all the same length.

Calendar:

- ☐ Complete the calendar.
- ☐ Review on back of calendar.

There are 4 sides to a square, so let's count to 4.

4

Application:

A folded t-shirt is like a square.

1

4   2

3

Count the sides of the square.

As you count slide your finger down each side.

Can you count with me now?

A square is the same length on each side.

Critical Thinking:

Look at the square of paper clips. To make sure each side is equal, count the paper clips on one side.

Now let's count how many paper clips we have on another side. Touch them as we count out loud. One, two, three, four.

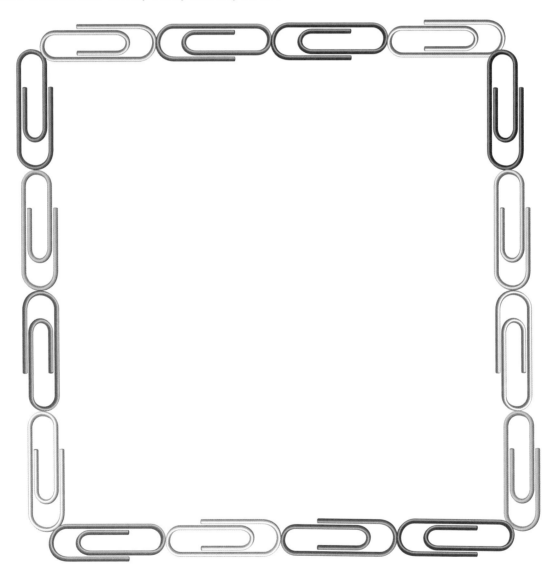

I had _____ paper clips on this side, and you have _____ paper clips on that side. That is the same number of paper clips, and that means that the sides are equal or the same length.

Application:

Trace the squares and count how many there are. Be sure you touch each square when counting.

Critical Thinking:

Using the shapes you have learned (circle, oval, triangle, and square), make a cat like this:

Great job!

7

There are 7 days in a week. Count to 7.

Application:

Remember, this is a square. It has 4 sides that are the same length.

Now count the following squares as you trace them.

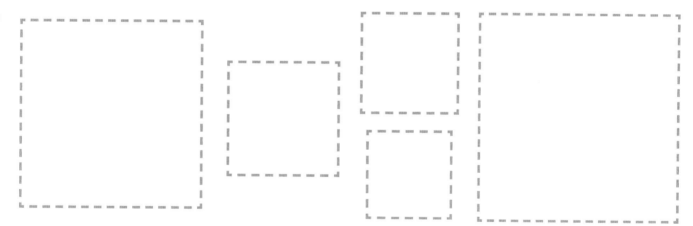

Let's see if you can make a square!

Teacher

If it is not raining, take your child outside to allow them to draw a square in the dirt or use sidewalk chalk or make a square with gravel or leaves. If it is raining, try to find something like round oat cereal or beans to use to make a square.

Critical Thinking:

Let's go on a Shape Hunt! Go around the house and see if you can find things that are square-shaped.

Application:

Mark the squares.

Critical Thinking:

Help Charlie and Charlotte count the rainy day things in the picture.

There are 7 days in a week. Count to 7.

7

Application:

Where do the shapes belong?

Match the shape with the correct toy bin it belongs in by drawing a line from each shape to the bin.

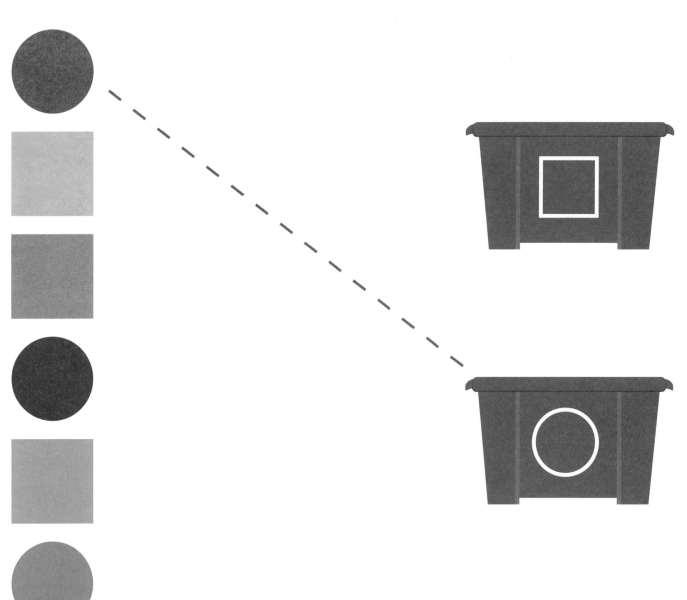

Critical Thinking:

Let's measure shapes!

Comparisons, Rectangles, and Shape Review

"Mama, is there anything else we can help you with?" Charlotte asked. They had helped fold Daddy's shirts and had matched a whole basket of his work socks. The whole time, Mom had talked to them about being kind and considerate. They had both apologized to each other and to Mom, for acting mean to each other during play time. The twins were happy that their mom explained to them that everyone gets angry sometimes; it was about what they did with that angry feeling that was important. It was important to choose kindness.

"Sure! There is a load of bed sheets and bath towels in the dryer. They are probably done by now. Why don't you two go and bring up that load while I go make us some lunch?" Mom instructed.

The twins grabbed the empty clothes basket and scampered down the basement steps. After piling the fresh-smelling sheets and towels into the basket, they each grabbed a handle and lugged it back up the stairs and into the family room, before skipping into the kitchen for lunch. Mom had made peanut butter and jam sandwiches, cut them in half, and placed one on a plate for each of them, adding a little bowl of applesauce and some carrot sticks to each plate to round out the meal.

"Charlotte, you can move that stack of kitchen towels off of the table. Just put them on Daddy's chair for now, so we can eat lunch." Charlotte carefully moved the stack of towels and dishcloths as her mother had instructed.

"Mmmmm. Yummy!" Charlie sighed happily as he took a huge bite of his applesauce. It had been made from the apples grown on his grandparents' farm.

"Mama, what is this shape?" Charlotte asked, studying her sandwich half. She knew it wasn't a square because it wasn't the same on all sides. Her sandwich had two longer sides and two shorter ones.

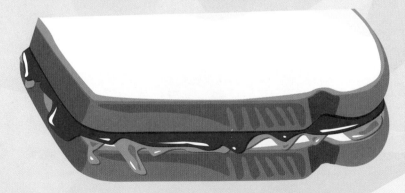

"That's a rectangle, Charlotte," Mom smiled at her daughter. "Look, I fold my kitchen towels into rectangles. See how they are different from the shape of Daddy's folded t-shirts?" Mom held up a folded kitchen towel from the stack of clean laundry on the chair next to her. "After lunch, I'll show you how we fold our bath towels into rectangles so they will fit nicely into the towel closet."

Calendar:

☐ Complete the calendar.

☐ Review on back of calendar.

Application:

Charlie and Charlotte noticed that a door has 4 sides, but 2 sides are short and 2 sides are long. This is called a rectangle.

Look at a door.
It is a rectangle.

This is also a rectangle.

How many sides does a rectangle have?

How many long sides?

How many short sides?

It has 4 sides; 2 sides are long and 2 sides are short. Do you count that, too?
See how many more rectangles you can find in the room you are in.

How many did you find?

Critical Thinking:

Teacher

Gather a few objects or toys for a tall/short, big/small comparison activity.

A giraffe is tall. It is taller than Charlie. Charlie is shorter than the giraffe.

A bear is big, but a mouse is small.

Look at the objects that were gathered.

What things are big? What are small?

Circle the answer to the following questions:

Are you taller or shorter than a baby?

Are you taller or shorter than a car?

Application:

1. Trace the big square. This is the main part of your house.

2. Trace the triangle for the roof of your house.

3. For your door, trace the rectangle.

4. Trace the circle for your doorknob.

5. Trace the windows of the house.

6. Trace the grass around the house.

7. Trace the oval clouds in the sky.

8. Trace the circle in the top corner for the sun.

   Good job!

Critical Thinking:

Let's Draw!

See if you can do the same house drawing without the tracing lines.

1. Draw a square starting at the dot on the page. This is the main part of your house.

2. Draw a triangle for the roof of your house.

3. For your door, draw a rectangle.

4. You need a circle for your doorknob.

5. Add windows of any shape you choose.

6. Add grass around the house.

7. Add 5 oval-shaped clouds.

8. Add a circle in the top corner for the sun.

Application:

Circle the smaller red fruits. Circle the larger green and yellow fruits. Circle the smaller purple and brown fruits.

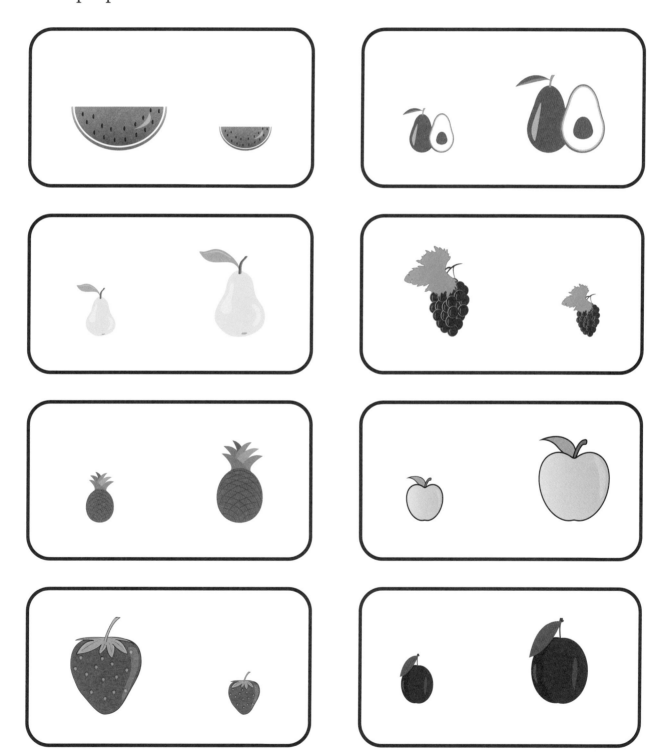

Remember how we learned what a rectangle is? Trace the rectangles:

How many rectangles do you have in all?

Critical Thinking:

Which rectangle is tallest?

Which rectangle is shortest?

Which rectangle is widest?

Which rectangle is smallest?

Application:

Connect the dots to make a rectangle.

Extra Fun:

- Make rectangles with playdough.
- Find rectangles in your pantry or cabinet.

Critical Thinking:

1. Put an X on the dog that is shortest.

2. Circle the dog that is tallest.

3. Put a square on the dogs that are both little.

4. Place a triangle on the dog that is widest.

Name_____

Application:

Charlie and Charlotte learned that a towel is a shape called a rectangle.

Do you see how a towel is like a rectangle? It has 2 short sides and 2 long sides.

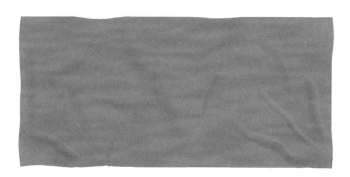

Can you draw a rectangle below?

Critical Thinking:

Teacher

Practice using things around you to ask which is bigger or smaller, and who is taller or shorter.

Look at these images. Draw a circle around the tallest object. Draw a square around the shortest object. Draw a circle around the biggest creature.

Comparisons, Stars, and Number Line

"The grass is so wet! It's squishing through my toes," Charlie looked down at his bare feet. It was getting so dark outside he could barely see them at all! He and Charlotte were out looking for fireflies. The early summer evening was cool, and the sun had just said "Good night" before slipping over the horizon.

Just at that moment, Charlotte and Daddy came around the side of the garage. Each of them held a jar with a lid that had holes punched in it. The twins and their dad had decided at supper that this evening would be the perfect time to go firefly watching. And just maybe, they would be lucky enough to capture one so they could observe it up close. They had learned that to observe something, they had to look closely and pay attention to the details. The jars would allow them to do this with a firefly without causing it any harm, and of course they would return the creature to its freedom after they were done with their observations.

"Look!" Charlotte shouted, pointing to a bright light right above the treeline. "Is it a firefly, Daddy?" Charlie came running to see what his sister had found. Dad scooped up Charlotte to make her as tall as himself. His

eyes followed to where she was pointing. "No, Charlotte, that's not a firefly; you've spotted the first star of the evening!"

"But how can that be a star? It's so tiny! You said that stars are huge — gigantic, Daddy! When you read us the story of the star that led those men to Jesus when He was a little child, you said that star was really, really big." Charlotte was confused.

Dad set her down on the ground again. "You're right, Honey. I did say that, and they are really big. But that star up there," Daddy pointed at the tiny bright spot in the sky, "that star is far, far, far away. That's why it looks so small. If we were closer to it, it would look much bigger!" Charlotte nodded. She was beginning to understand.

"Look, Dad! There's another star!" shouted Charlie.

"Actually, Charlie, that's a little firefly! Come on, guys, let's see if we can catch it!" The three of them scampered through the wet grass after the twinkling light, until they collapsed into a giggling heap on the ground. Their firefly observations would have to wait for another evening. Overhead, millions of seemingly tiny stars twinkled in the night sky.

Calendar:

☐ Complete the calendar.

☐ Review on back of calendar.

Application:

A star is a unique shape. It has 10 sides and 5 points and looks like this.

Count each point on the star.

A star in the sky seems teeny tiny to us because it is so far away, but most stars are actually very big! The sun is a star, and it is definitely VERY big. Can you think of something that is teeny tiny or VERY small?

Critical Thinking:

Robot Challenge:

Look at the robot made of shapes.

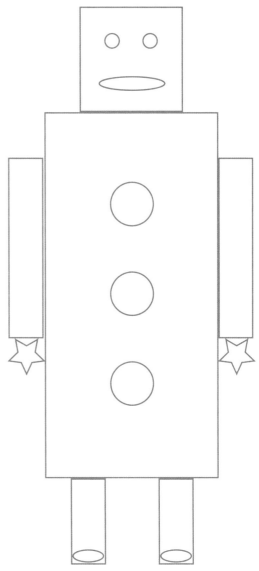

Using the shapes of the robot, answer these questions:

Which shape is teeny tiny?

Which shape is big?

What is something shorter than the robot?

Where are the stars on the robot?

How many rectangles are on the robot?

Application:

Did you know that the Bible speaks a lot about stars? The Book of Philippians (2:14–15) even says we are like stars or lights when we live for God.

Do all things without complaining and disputing, that you may become blameless and harmless, children of God without fault in the midst of a crooked and perverse generation, among whom you shine as lights in the world…

Trace the star below.

Critical Thinking:

Let's count stars.

Can you count how many blue stars there are?

What about yellow stars?

How many red stars do you see?

Application:

Color the night scene.

Critical Thinking:

Using your night scene picture on the previous page:

Count how many stars you have on your night scene.

How many do you see?

How many birds do you see?

Application:

Using painter's tape or post-it notes, make a number line from 0–5.

Hop from 0–5 as you count. Place an object on each number. How many do you have?

Critical Thinking:

Trace the stars with your finger and count them as you do.

Application:

Circle the items that are big. Place an X on the items that are tiny.

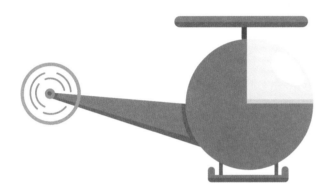

Critical Thinking:

Using toothpicks, make star shapes on the table like the one below.

Opposites and Symmetry

"I'm so full, I could pop!" Charlie rubbed his tummy and pushed his chair back from the table. "Those were really good pancakes, Mom."

Charlotte used her last piece of bacon to sop up the syrup left on her plate. She loved how the salty bacon and sweet maple syrup tasted together. Sweet and salty, and oh so yummy! She remembered how Grandma had explained to her and Charlie that the little bumps on their tongues sent information about how things taste up to their brains. Grandma had explained that this was their sense of taste, and it was just one of their five senses. Charlotte thought it was amazing that their tongues could tell their brains that something tasted good! She was thankful for her taste buds.

"May we go outside and play, Mama?" Charlotte asked as she carried her plate to the sink. "We want to find our first butterfly of the year today!"

"Yes, Mom, can we go outside and play? The sun is out now and it's really warm," Charlie joined in. He decided to follow his sister's example and took his plate to the sink, too.

"Sure. That's fine, but you two make sure that you don't get filthy. Remember, we have the church picnic later!" Mom replied. "And please stay in our yard — no playing on the sidewalk or driveway," she added. The children nodded happily and ran for their shoes.

"Charlie, let's swing first, okay?" Charlotte suggested as she carefully tied her left shoe.

"Okay! Then we can practice t-ball!" Charlie agreed. The twins both jumped to their feet and skipped out the back door and into their backyard. Swinging was one of their favorite outside activities.

Dad had shown them how to pump their legs to make their swing go higher. As they swung, they watched as their shadows followed them back and forth, back and forth. The sun was high overhead and the breeze was warm. Swinging was so much fun!

"Charlie, look! Our shadows look exactly like us! I mean, they are the same shape as us!" Charlotte pointed out. She swung her head back and forth, making her ponytails swing back and forth on both sides of her head — her shadow did the same. Just then, a beautiful blue butterfly landed on the lilac bush near the swing set. The first butterfly of the summer!

Calendar:

☐ Complete the calendar.

☐ Review on back of calendar.

Application:

Did you notice how Charlie and Charlotte were eating and they tasted something salty and something sweet? Those are what we call **opposites**. Another opposite would be out and in.

Match the opposites:

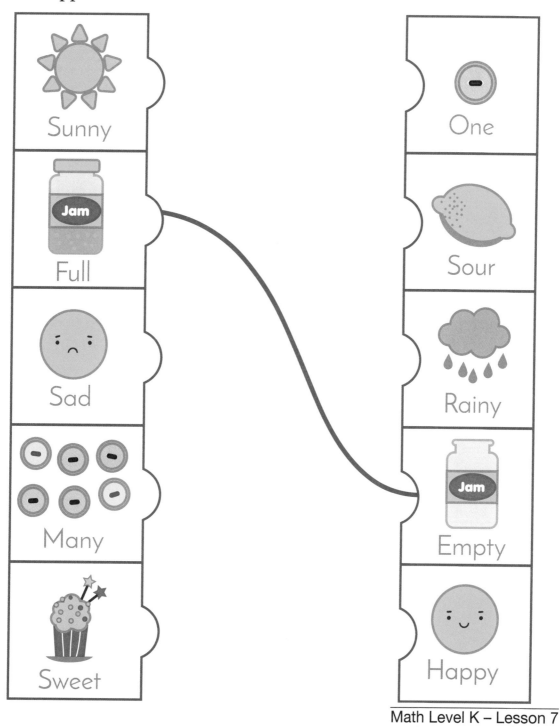

Critical Thinking:

Charlie and Charlotte also noticed their shadows.

Look at this shadow.

What does this shadow look like?

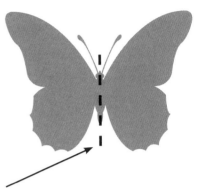

If we draw a line down the middle of the shadow from top to bottom, then we have the same thing on each side. This is called **symmetry**. We have symmetry too. We have an ear on each side, one eye on each side, and an arm on each side. This means we are symmetrical.

Make a line on each shadow to divide it in half to show the symmetry.

Application:

Can you think of the opposite of up? (down)

What is the opposite of light? (dark)

If you are little, then I am what? (big)

If a giraffe is tall, then you are what? (short)

Draw a line to connect the opposites:

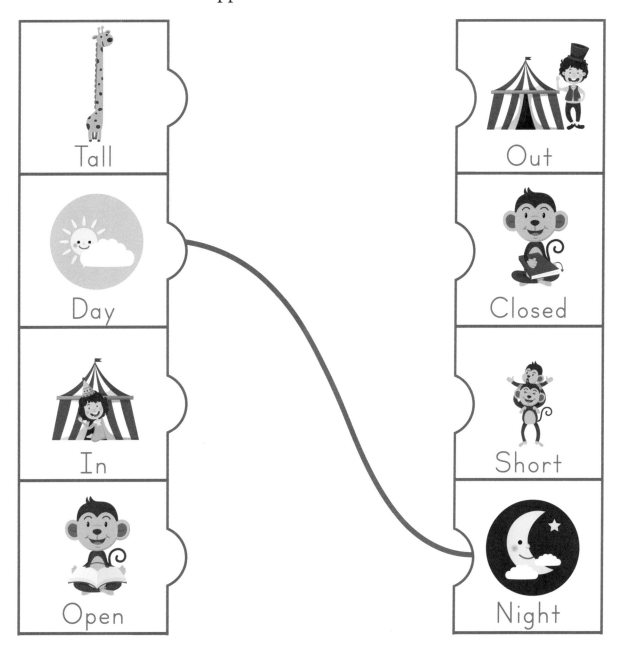

Critical Thinking:

Opposites Game:

I am going to say a word or phrase, and you are going to say the opposite!

Up

Running fast

Smile

Sit

Draw a line to show symmetry on the images below.

Application:

Match the opposites:

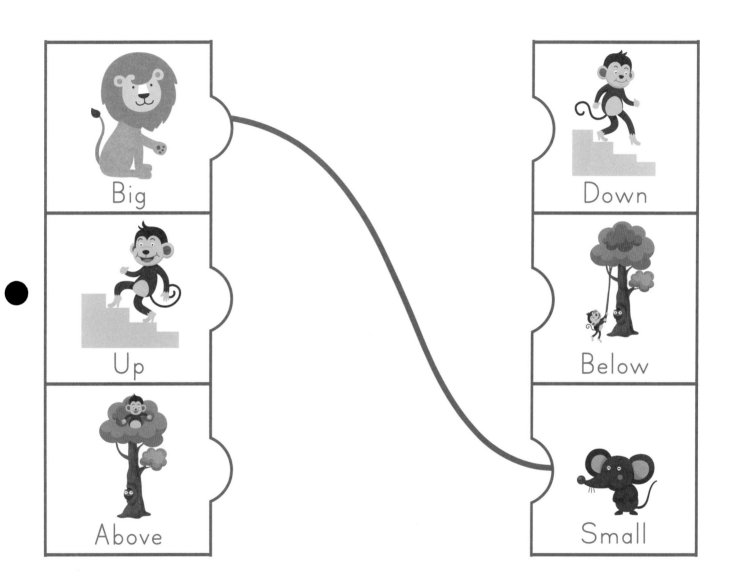

Critical Thinking:

Oh no! The spider and butterfly are not symmetrical. Draw the missing half to make them have symmetry again.

Application:

Search and find game:

The coffee table is hard. Search and find something soft.

The fire in the fireplace is hot. Search and find something that is cold.

The book is inside. Search and find something that is outside.

The clock is up. Search and find something that is down.

Critical Thinking:

Match the other half of the shape to make it symmetrical.

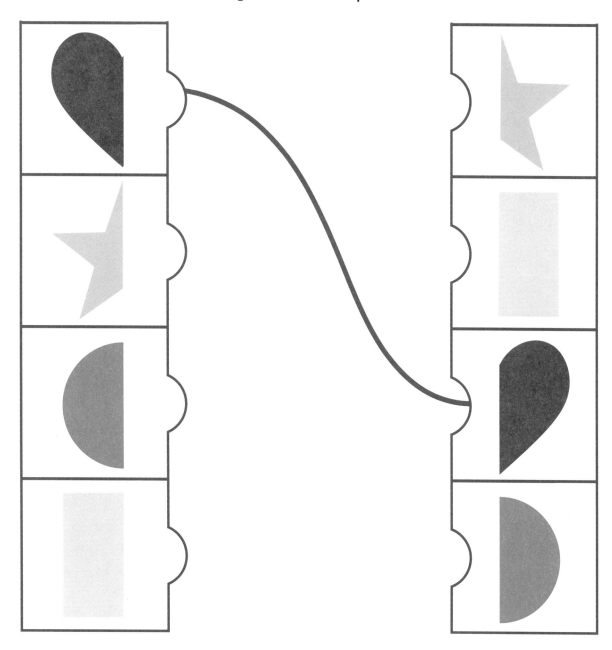

Application:

Match the opposites.

Critical Thinking:

Draw shapes to make the butterfly symmetrical.

Differences and Similarities, and Matching

"Daddy, can we go play with Jennifer and Jason?" Charlie asked, hopping from one foot to the other. "Their family is right over there." He pointed to a family setting up their picnic table a few tables away from theirs.

"Sure, Charlie, but you two make sure that you stay where Mom and I can see you at all times. Understood?" The twins nodded and ran off to find their friends. They loved the annual church picnic. There were so many children to play with, and so many yummy pies and cakes to taste. The children met up with Jennifer and Jason, and together they skipped over to the tables where all of the yummy food was being arranged to look at the pies and cakes.

One entire table was full of pies. The children walked slowly down the length of the table, studying each one carefully. There were blueberry pies with fancy lattice top crusts. There were beautiful chocolate cream pies with fluffy, white whipped cream and curly, chocolate shavings. There were simple pumpkin pies with crimped bottom crusts and a sprinkle of cinnamon on the top.

The twins spotted the pie that their mama had made. It was a gorgeous, fresh strawberry pie. The bright red strawberries were mounded high. This was the twins' favorite kind of pie! Their mama's beautiful strawberry pie was the only one like it at the picnic. The twins thought it was the most beautiful, too! Some of the other pies looked the same. All of the apple pies had pretty cutouts in their top crusts, all of the lemon-meringue were bright yellow with peaks of white on top, and all of the pumpkin pies had wavy crust edges. These were all the same.

Charlie and Charlotte were learning to observe things around them very carefully. Mama had taught them how to look closely at details and how to use those details to organize or match things. For example, when the children were helping fold laundry, they had to be very careful and observant when they matched socks. Even if two socks were the same color, this did not mean they were a matching pair. They could be the same color but not the same height or size. For them to match, they had to be exactly the same! One time, Charlie had matched one of his small dark blue socks with Daddy's big dark blue sock. This had not worked too well!

Calendar:

☐ Complete the calendar.

☐ Review on back of calendar.

Application:

Not all objects look the same, do they?

These are the same.

These are different because of the patterns on them and their colors.

Which ball is a different shape? Put an X on the one that is differently shaped.

Critical Thinking:

Match the object to the shape that is the same as it is:

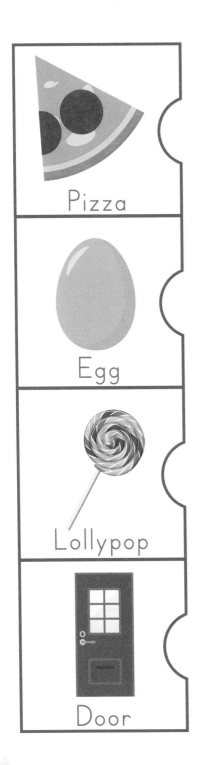

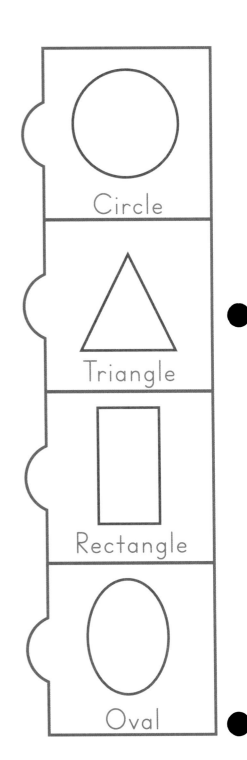

Application:

Which one is the same? Circle the one that is the same as the other in each row.

Critical Thinking:

Can you spot the difference? <u>Hint</u>: There are 6.

Application:

This sock is the same as this sock. They belong together.

This sock is different from this sock. They do not belong together.

Search and find 2 objects that are the same or belong together.

Search and find 1 object that is different or does not belong with the others.

Critical Thinking:

Can you spot the differences? <u>Hint:</u> There are 8.

Application:

Same or different? Circle the one that is the same as the other.

Critical Thinking:

Which one is different or does not belong? Circle it.

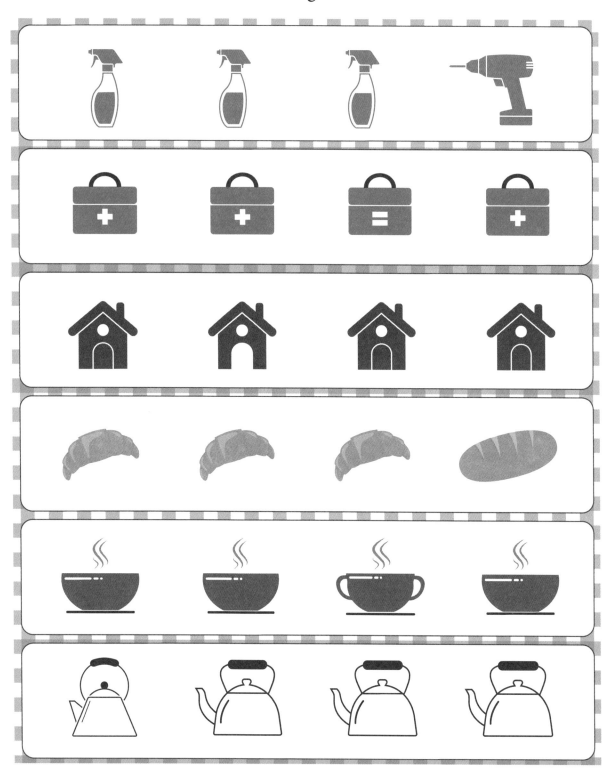

Application:

Circle the one that is different or does not belong in each row.

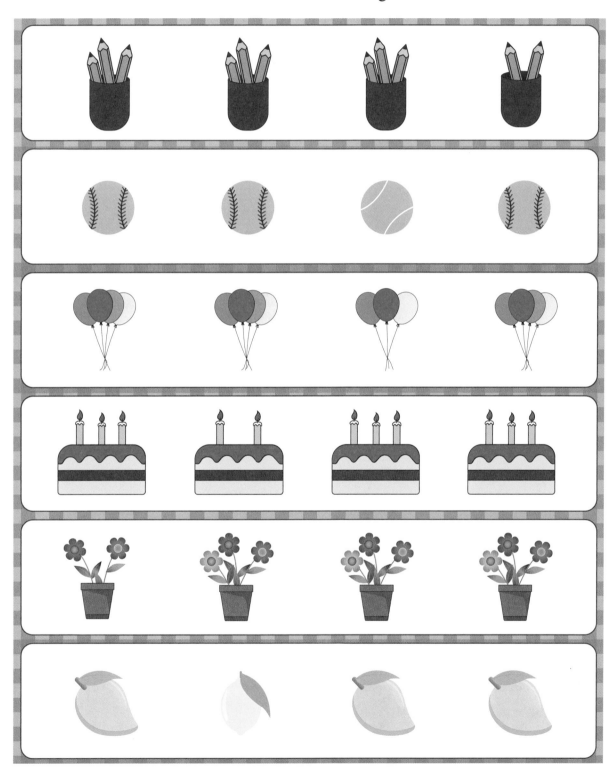

Critical Thinking:

Which one is different or does not belong? Circle it.

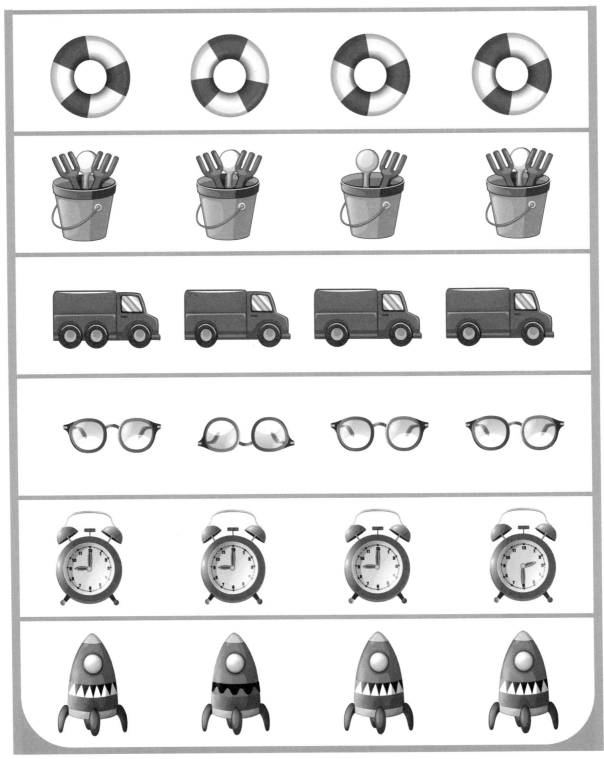

Cooking and Measuring, Diamonds, and Graphing

"Okay, you two, I need your help." Mom steered Charlie and Charlotte over to a table that had apple samples. The family was visiting an apple orchard, and the twins had never seen so many kinds of apple trees. They had picked apples from the five trees at their grandparents' farm, but those were all of the same kind of apples. This orchard had rows and rows and rows of trees as far as the children could see! "I am going to buy two bushels of apples to make apple sauce and pie filling," Mom explained to the children. "You each taste these and tell me which ones you like best."

"Mmmm! I like that one!" Charlotte declared. "It's just right. Not too sweet and not too sour . . . or tart."

"Oh, I like this one!" Charlie pointed to a large, pinkish apple. He had never seen an apple that color. The orchard worker told them that it was named "Pink Lady." The twins thought that was a funny name for a piece of fruit.

When the family got home after their orchard adventure, the twins helped Mom sort the apples by kind. They made sure that they placed any apples that had bruises or bad spots on the table so Mom could use those first. She said that she would make an apple crisp for dessert tonight and the twins could help her.

After the sorting was finished, Charlie and Charlotte helped Mom measure out the right amounts of flour, sugar, cinnamon, nutmeg, salt, and rolled oats for the apple crisp. As the family enjoyed their delicious dessert, the children decided that they had never tasted anything better.

Calendar:

☐ Complete the calendar.

☐ Review on back of calendar.

Application:

See this shape here:

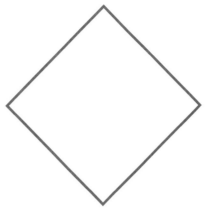

This is what we call a diamond. Notice how a diamond is kind of like a square? It has 4 sides, but they do not always have to be equal. It also looks like a kite!

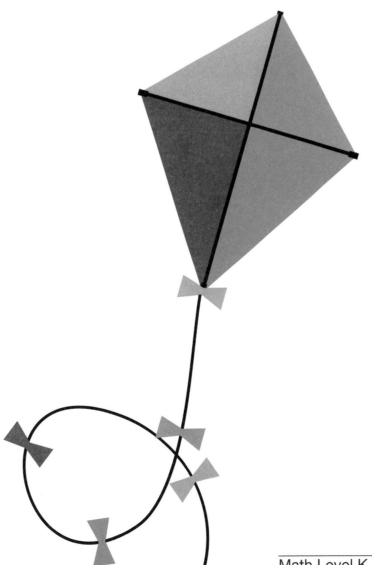

Critical Thinking:

Today, we are measuring fruit and nuts. When we measure, we fill our measuring cup to the top. This equals 1 cup. We have other measuring cups that are less than this and some that are more. We might use one that says it is ½ cup or ¼ cup, but today we are measuring 1 cup.

> **Teacher**
>
> *Using raisins, nuts, and dried fruit, make trail mix using 1 cup of each.*
>
> *Help students measure out 1 cup of each.*

Application:

Do you remember what shape this is?

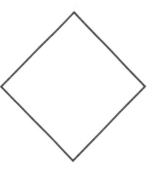

Remember, diamonds have 4 sides, but all sides do not have to be the same length.

Today, we will trace the shape to make a kite. A kite is also a diamond.

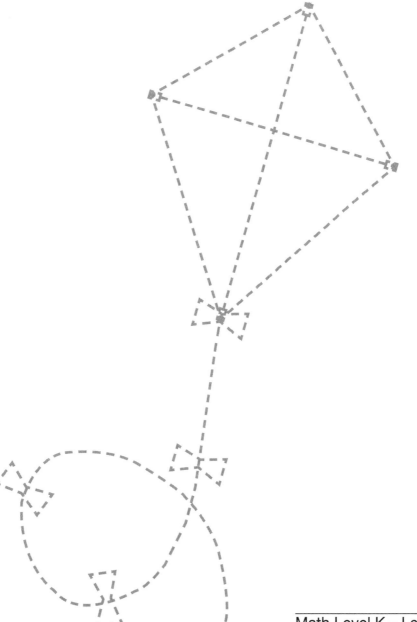

Critical Thinking:

Tasting apples:

Try 3 different apples. Have everyone in your family (or class) taste the apples, too.

Have each person vote on which one was their favorite apple by placing a post-it note in a container in front of each type of apple. Place 3 post-its in the one you liked the most, 2 post-its in the one you like somewhat, and 1 post-it in the one you like the least.

Teacher

We will continue this more tomorrow.

Application:

Use toothpicks or pencils to make a diamond shape. Count the sides and tell your teacher how many you have.

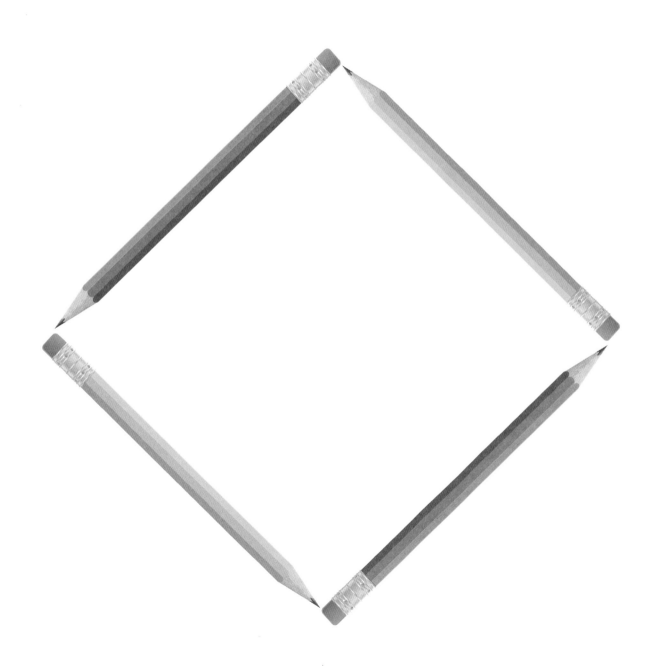

Critical Thinking:

Using the information you gathered yesterday, fill in the graph below:

Which apple had the most votes? Count how many votes it had.

Which one had the least?

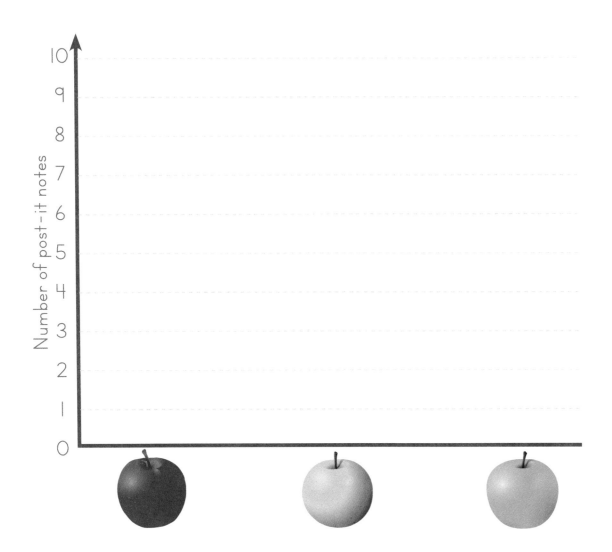

Application:

Find and color the diamonds:

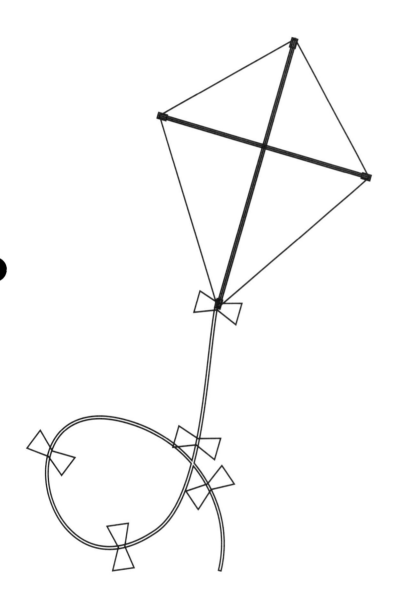 

Critical Thinking:

Recipe

Cooking Apple Dumplings:

Ingredients:

2 granny smith apples, cut into eighths and peeled

½ stick butter, melted

1 cup sugar

2 packages of crescent rolls

9 x 13 cake pan

1 tablespoon cinnamon

Teacher

Allow students to do as much as you feel they are capable of doing. The teacher may want to turn on the oven and should take the hot pan from the oven.

Preheat oven to 350°. Take each triangle of the crescent roll and wrap it around one slice of apple and seal it around the apple. Do this for all 16 triangles and apple slices.

Place them evenly in a cake pan, not touching each other (1 inch apart is good).

In a separate bowl, mix the melted butter, sugar, and cinnamon together.

Pour this mixture over each dumpling, making sure each one has some on it.

Bake for 45 minutes or until golden brown.

Enjoy!

Application:

Trace the diamonds, then draw your own. Count how many there are.

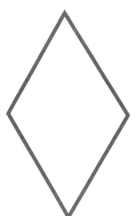  

Look at the graph about the cats and dogs at the animal shelter.

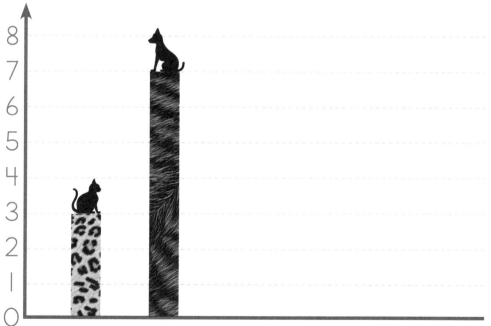

Are there more cats or more dogs?

How many cats are there?

Critical Thinking:

Prompt them with the questions.

Which one holds more than all the rest?

Which one holds the least or not as much as all the rest?

Teacher

Allow the student to play with water and measuring cups of ¼ cup, ½ cup, and 1 cup.

Number of the Week: 0, Measuring, and Counting Review

"Daddy, why are some of the tomatoes red and some green?" Charlotte asked as she carefully moved her basket down the row of green beans. She and Charlie were helping their dad work in the garden. They had helped weed the sugar snap peas, and now they were picking some green beans for supper, while Dad picked some tomatoes for their elderly neighbors, Frank and Cathy Reynolds.

"The green ones are not ripe yet, Charlotte," Dad answered before adding, "and the red ones are the ones we usually pick to eat. But tonight, we're going to do something different! Have you two ever tried fried green tomatoes?" When the twins looked at each other questioningly, Dad explained further, "Fried green tomatoes are a dish that Mama doesn't care for, but I really like! You two get to decide if you like them or not because I'm going to make some tonight! Can you two finish picking the green beans? I'm going to take these tomatoes over to Mr. and Mrs. Reynolds' house. I'll be back in a few minutes." The children nodded and continued picking the green beans.

When their dad returned, Charlie and Charlotte stood back and admired their work. There were small baskets and buckets full of bright green sugar snap peas, light yellow summer squash, bright red heirloom tomatoes, dark red cherry tomatoes, and two royal purple eggplants. The produce was a beautiful array of colors.

Inside the house, Dad wrapped a dish towel around each of the children's waists and helped them stand on chairs that he had pulled over to the kitchen counter. Dad instructed Charlie to scoop up two cups of yellow cornmeal into a large mixing bowl, and he gave Charlotte the task of measuring 2 teaspoons salt, ½ teaspoon pepper, and ½ teaspoon paprika to the mixture, while he carefully sliced 2 firm, green tomatoes into even slices. Next, he cracked 2 eggs into another bowl and whisked them until they were beaten well. Charlie and Charlotte watched as their dad carefully dipped each slice of tomato into the egg and then into the dry mixture before placing it into the hot oil in the frying pan. The twins both wondered if they were going to like this interesting dish — fried green tomatoes. It sure smelled good!

Calendar:

☐ Complete the calendar.

☐ Review on back of calendar.

Application:

Number of the Week: 0 — Z-E-R-O spells zero.

This is the number 0. If we have zero books, we have none.

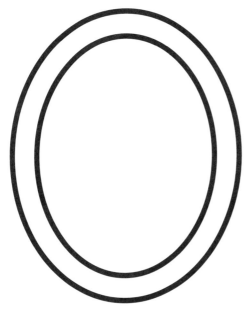

When we write a 0, we start at the top:

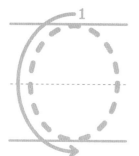

"Over around and close, that's the way to make zero."

Trace the 0's.

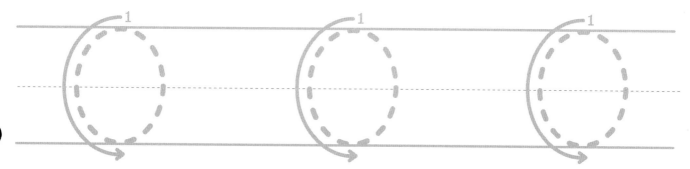

Critical Thinking:

Fruit or not?

If the picture in the box is a fruit, circle the thumbs up. If not, circle the thumbs down.

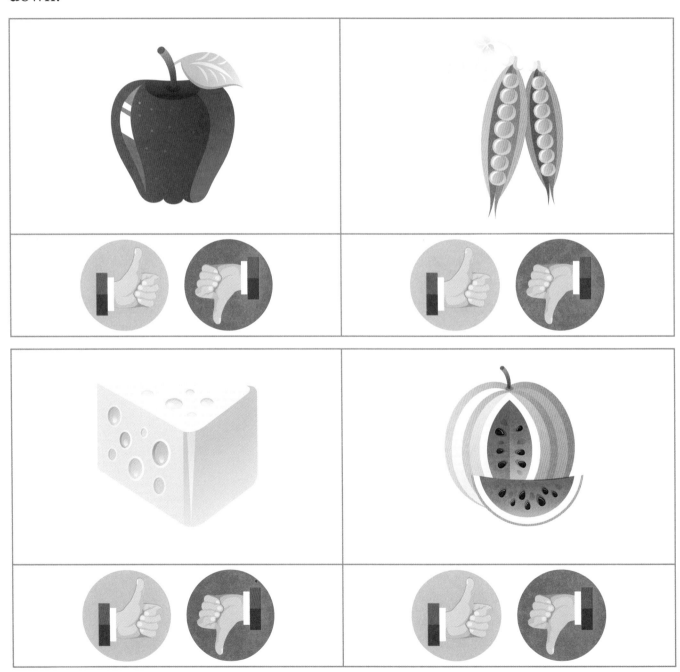

Application:

Number of the Week: 0 — Z-E-R-O spells zero.

This is the number 0. If we have zero books, we have none. When we write a 0, we start at the top:

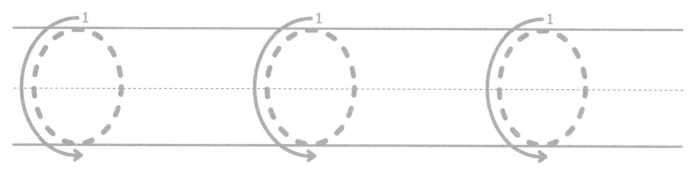

"Over around and close, that's the way to make zero."

Trace the 0's.

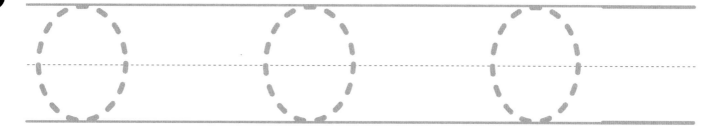

Teacher

Review: Using colored toothpicks and a toothpick dispenser with a lid with small holes, complete this activity.

Count out 5 toothpicks. Put them into the holes of the lid of the dispenser.

Continuing doing this as you tell your teacher the color of the toothpicks.

Critical Thinking:

Measuring Cup Play:

I wonder how many scoops of this cup you can put into this one? I wonder how many teaspoons you can put in this tablespoon? Or in the cup?

Application:

Number of the Week: 0 — Z-E-R-O spells zero.

This is the number 0. Zero means none. When we write a 0, we start at the top:

"Over around and close, that's the way to make zero."

Trace the 0's.

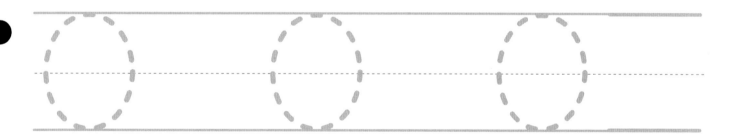

The foods are sorted by color. Count how many foods are in each color.

Critical Thinking:

Make wedding cookies or your favorite cookie made by scratch.

Here is a recipe:

Recipe

Wedding Cookies:

Ingredients:

1 ½ cup unsalted butter

¾ cup powdered sugar

¾ teaspoon salt

1½ cup ground or finely chopped pecans

4 ½ teaspoons vanilla

3 cups flour

Teacher

The teacher will want to turn on the oven and should take the hot pan from the oven.

Preheat oven to 325°. Cream the butter with sugar and salt. Mix in pecans and vanilla. Gradually blend in the flour. Roll into balls and place on cookie sheet at least 1 inch apart. Bake 15–20 minutes; do not brown.

Cool slightly. Roll them or sprinkle them in powdered sugar.

Application:

Number of the Week: 0 — Z-E-R-O spells zero.

This is the number 0. Zero means none. When we write a 0, we start at the top:

"Over around and close, that's the way to make zero."

Trace the 0's.

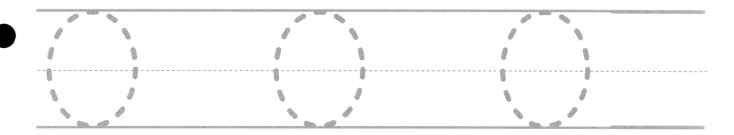

Go outside and count five leaves from two trees OR count 5 toys and 5 books.

Critical Thinking:

Where does it belong?

Sort the food where it belongs. Draw a line to where the food product belongs: the refrigerator or the pantry.

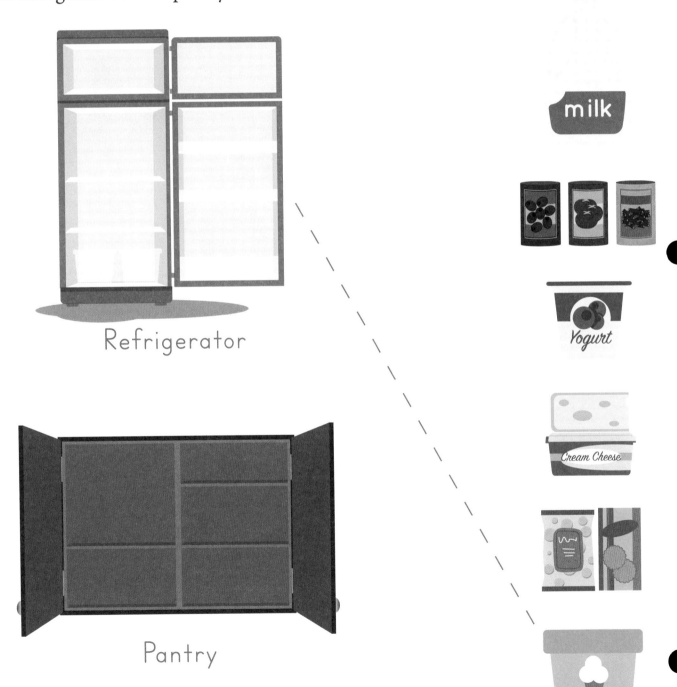

Application:

Number of the Week: 0 — Z-E-R-O spells zero

This is the number 0. Zero means none. When we write a 0, we start at the top:

"Over around and close, that's the way to make zero."

Trace the 0's.

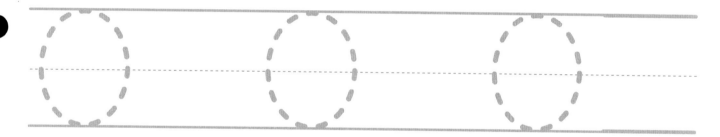

Color the objects and count how many there are in each row.

Critical Thinking:

Circle the measuring cup that is biggest:

Circle the measuring spoon that is smallest:

"The LORD our God, the LORD is one!" Pastor Donovan's voice rang out. "Yes, He is one!" answered the congregation. It was a beautiful, clear Sunday morning. The twins and their parents were worshiping together as they sat side by side in the sanctuary of their church. Both Charlie and Charlotte loved the atmosphere of their church. Everyone was friendly and the singing was beautiful. Today was a special day because there was a guest speaker — a missionary who served with their church's support in Papua New Guinea, an island nation located near Australia and New Zealand.

As the missionary told the congregation about the mighty acts of God that were happening in Papua New Guinea, the twins listened quietly. Their parents had shown them on a map where the missionaries lived. They had also shown the children pictures of the people who lived there, as well as the animals from that area. Charlie and Charlotte thought it was fascinating!

When they got home, Charlie wanted to see again where Papua New Guinea was. "Let's get a map book out and find it again," their dad said. Charlie ran to get it, and he and Charlotte watched as their dad found the pages for the island nation.

"Let's play a game to see if you can find it with some position word clues," their dad said.

"What's that?" asked Charlotte.

"Well," their dad began, "you two begin pointing to the map and telling me where you think it is, and I'll give you clue words like above or below to help you. Are you ready?"

"Yes!" they both said together, very excited to solve the mystery. They both reached out to the map and pointed at an area of countries on the page known as Asia.

"That is pretty close," their dad said, "but you are pointing above Papua New Guinea. Try again." He smiled as they started pointing down and down on the map, ending up on Australia. "Ah, now you're pointing just a little below the country."

Charlie and Charlotte both slowly moved their fingers up slightly until they were both pointing to a large island just above Australia. "There!" their dad shouted. "Now you are pointing directly on the country!" They all just began laughing at his excitement for them.

Calendar:

☐ Complete the calendar.

☐ Review on back of calendar.

Application:

Number of the Week: 1 — O-N-E spells one.

This is the number 1. Count the pumpkin.

When we write a 1, we start at the top:

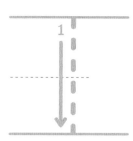

"Straight down, then you're done, that's the way we make a 1."

Trace the 1's.

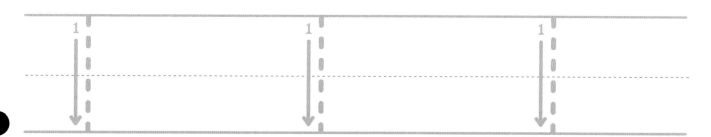

Critical Thinking:

Today, we will learn words that show positions.

Here is an example:

The dog is **IN** the house.   The dog is **ON** the house.

The dog is **BESIDE** the house.

Let's play a game using a toy.

I will ask you to put your toy in different places and we will see if you can put it in the right spot.

· Put the toy on the table.

· Put the toy beside the table.

· Put the toy in your room.

Application:

Number of the Week: 1 — O-N-E spells one.

"Straight down, then you're done, that's the way we make a 1."

Show me one finger. Trace the 1's.

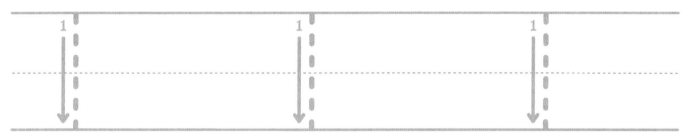

Today, we will learn some more words that show positions. Here is another example:

The sun is **ABOVE** the house.

The cloud is **BELOW** the sun.

The flower is **BETWEEN** the house and the tree.

Critical Thinking:

We will play another game using a toy.

Hold the toy above the table.

Put the toy below the table.

Place the toy between the books.

Application:

Number of the Week: 1 — O-N-E spells one.

This is the number 1. There is one stick horse.

"Straight down, then you're done, that's the way we make a 1."

Show me one finger. Trace the 1's.

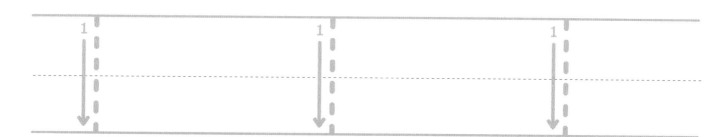

Critical Thinking:

Draw a circle **ABOVE** the barn.

Put a tire swing **BELOW** the tree.

Draw a chick **BETWEEN** the chickens.

Place an X **ON** the barn.

Draw a duck **IN** the water.

Draw a bird **BESIDE** the tree.

Application:

Number of the Week: 1 — O-N-E spells one.

This is the number 1. There is one wind-up dinosaur.

"Straight down, then you're done, that's the way we make a 1."

Show me one finger. Trace the 1's.

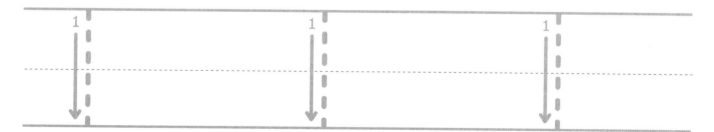

Teacher

Optional: Use the position words for having them put items away (toys in the toy bin, pillow on your bed, etc.).

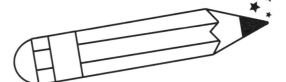

Circle each number one.

1 4 1 8 2

2 1 3 6 1

5 9 1 4 7

1 3 2 1 1

Application:

Number of the Week: 1 — O-N-E spells one.

"Straight down, then you're done, that's the way we make a 1."

Show me one finger. Trace the 1's.

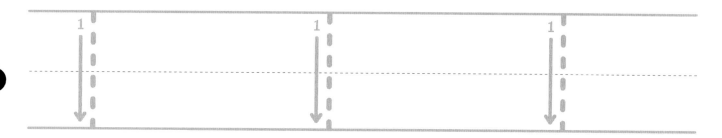

Circle the items with 1 in the group.

Critical Thinking:

Tell where Charlie and Charlotte are in the tree. Draw a circle on the child who is above. Draw a square on the child who is below.

above

below

Number of the Week: 2, and Position Words

"Charlotte, can you grab that side of the sheet and tuck it *under* the mattress . . . like this?" Mom instructed Charlotte, while showing her how to tuck the edge of the sheet under the mattress on the guest room bed. Grandma and Grandpa were coming later that afternoon, and Mom wanted the bedding to be clean and fresh for their visit. Charlotte tugged the edge of the fitted sheet *over* the corner and under the edge of the mattress as Mom instructed.

Next, they spread the top sheet *on top of* the fitted sheet, smoothing out the wrinkles and making sure that the sides were hanging evenly on either side. Next, they fluffed up the 2, freshly laundered pillows and slipped them into clean pillow cases. As the finishing touch, they spread a brightly colored quilt over the bed, placing 2 decorative pillows *in front of* the 2 larger bed pillows.

"Charlie, can you please dust in here? Just run the dusting rag *behind* all of the pictures on that dresser, in front of the knick-knacks on that shelf . . . and put that box of odds and ends *under* the bed. Then I think we're all done!" Mom wiped her hands down the sides of her jeans, tucked her hair *behind* her ear, and surveyed the room. Yes, everything looked tidy and fresh.

"Mama, are we going to do anything fun when Grandma and Grandpa are here?" Charlotte asked as they ate their lunch of macaroni and cheese and fresh green beans from the garden, together around the kitchen table.

"Well, Grandma bought tickets to go to a play at the children's theater. She said that it's a play called *Famous Nursery Rhymes*. So, that should be fun!" Mom answered before taking a bite of her lunch.

"Yay! That <u>is</u> going to be fun!" Charlie hooted in delight. "I wonder if one of the actors is going to dress like a cow and jump over a moon! Hehehe," he giggled behind his hand.

"Yeah, and maybe someone will dress like a cat and play a fiddle!" Charlotte added. "That would be so funny!" The twins were looking forward to this play!

Calendar:

☐ Complete the calendar.

☐ Review on back of calendar.

Application:

Number of the Week: 2 — T-W-O spells two.

This is the number 2. Count the 2 balls.

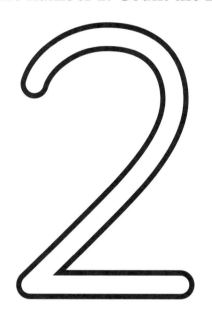

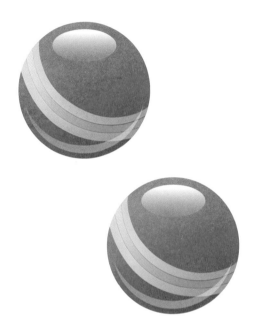

When we write a 2, we start near the top:

"Around and back on the track, that's the way we write a 2."

Trace the 2's:

Critical Thinking:

Teacher

Read Humpty Dumpty with your student.

Humpty Dumpty sat on a wall,
Humpty Dumpty had a great fall.
All the king's horses and all the king's men
Couldn't put Humpty together again.

Humpty Dumpty sat ON a wall. How can you sit on a wall?

The car farthest to the right is IN FRONT of the line.

IN FRONT of is what you're looking at straight ahead.

BEHIND means just the opposite. It is what is behind your head. So, this car IN FRONT has this car BEHIND it.

IN FRONT of is what you're looking at straight ahead, but behind is what you can't see behind your head.

Circle the picture that shows the cat IN FRONT of the box.

Circle the picture that shows the dog BEHIND the box.

Application:

Number of the Week: 2 — T-W-O spells two.

This is the number 2. When we write a 2, we start near the top:

"Around and back on the track, that's the way we write a 2."
Let's practice writing the numbers we have learned so far.

Let's trace these.

Circle only 2 objects.

Critical Thinking:

Read the rhyme Hey Diddle Diddle.

> Hey, diddle, diddle
> The cat and the fiddle
> The cow jumped over the moon
> The little dog laughed to see such sport
> And the dish ran away with the spoon.

We will be like the cow who jumped OVER the moon!

Teacher	*Lay out small objects for jumping over.*

Jump OVER each item.

Teacher	*Place a piece of paper under a book.*

Now, I want you to look, as I have put a piece of paper UNDER a book. Can you put the book under the table? Under is kind of like BELOW.

Application:

Number of the Week: 2 — T-W-O spells two.

This is the number 2. When we write a 2, we start near the top:

"Around and back on the track, that's the way we write a 2." Trace the 2's:

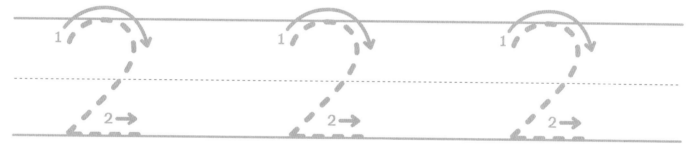

Circle the groups that have 2 objects:

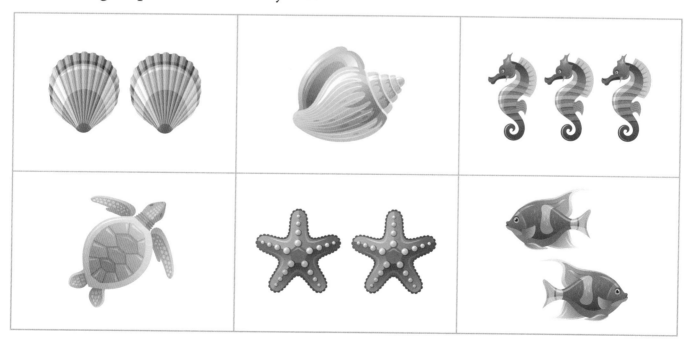

Critical Thinking:

Where are they? In front of or behind? Draw a line to show where they belong.

in front of

behind

Application:

Number of the Week: 2 — T-W-O spells two.

This is the number 2. When we write a 2, we start near the top:

"Around and back on the track, that's the way we write a 2."

Trace the 2's:

Find 2 of your favorite things and show them to your teacher. Hop and count to 2. Count 2 fingers.

Critical Thinking:

Match the description to the owl's position.

in front of

between

under

on

behind

beside

Application:

Number of the Week: 2 — T-W-O spells two.

This is the number 2. When we write a 2, we start near the top:

"Around and back on the track, that's the way we write a 2."

Trace the 2's:

Circle the two's:

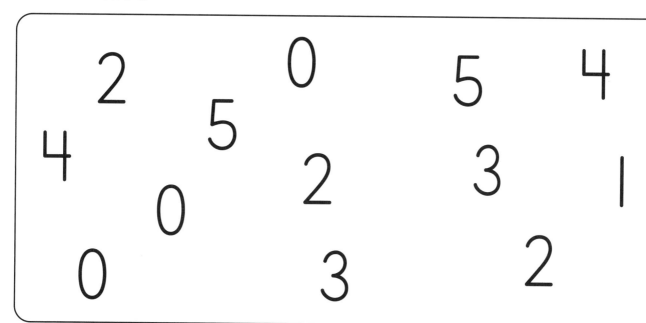

Critical Thinking:

Review of Position Words:

Point to the item in the picture that matches the word. Your teacher can mark them off as you say them.

above	between	in	over
below	on	beside	under
in front of	behind		

Number of the Week: 3, and More or Less

Charlie heard Charlotte laughing outside, so he quickly ran out to see what might be so funny. There she was jump roping, "Skip, skip, skip!" Her ponytails swung back and forth in time to her jumping, and she seemed so happy. "Come on, Charlie! Grab the other rope, and let's jump together!" She paused for a moment so he could get ready.

After Charlie picked up the other rope, they stood side-by-side and starting counting together: "One, two, three, jump!" They had learned that counting to 3 helped them jump at the exact same time.

The twins had been practicing their jump roping skills diligently. It was hard work to keep your feet going at the right speed and watch as the rope came around and around. They were both becoming very good at it, though, and had been learning new jump roping rhymes to help keep them going at the right speed. Some of the rhymes were funny, and some were riddles with answers that came at the end — if they didn't mess up before then! All of the chants and rhymes were very helpful in their practice, though. That evening at dinner, the children took turns telling their dad about their day.

"I jumped a lot of times today, Dad," Charlie declared, "but, Charlotte jumped more. She's really good at it!"

Charlotte smiled at her brother. "Thanks, Charlie!" she exclaimed. "But you're really good at jumping rope too! You spend a little less time practicing I think . . . Mom says that the more you practice, the better you get." Charlie nodded in agreement; he knew Charlotte spent more time than he did jumping rope.

"You two are talking about some very important concepts! More and less applies to many things in life," Dad explained. "For example, I eat more than Mom does, so we can say that she eats less. More and less are just one set of opposites that we see in life around us. Can you two think of any other opposites?"

"Yes! How about over and under? Or in front of and behind?" Charlie said.

"Oh, and above and below! And in and out!" Charlotte added. "Daddy, opposites kind of match, don't they? I mean they go together, like Charlie and me. He's a boy, and I'm a girl. We're opposite, but matching!"

Calendar:

☐ Complete the calendar.

☐ Review on back of calendar.

Application:

Number of the Week:

3 — T-H-R-E-E spells three.

This is the number 3. Count the 3 balloons.

 When we write a 3, we start near the top:

"Around the tree, around the tree, that's the way we make a 3."

Trace the 3's:

Color the number 3.

Critical Thinking:

Three is more than zero. Three is also more than one and more than two.

Which one has more? Circle it.

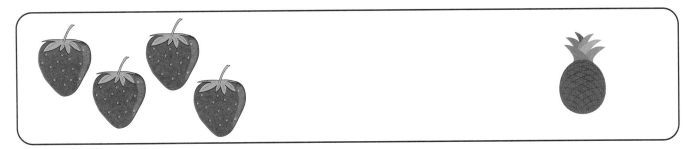

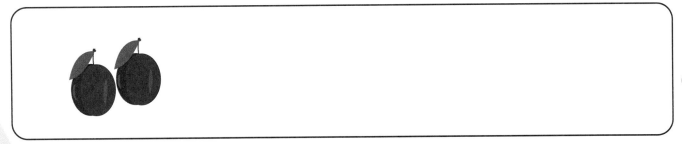

Application:

Number of the Week:

3 — T-H-R-E-E spells three.

Let's practice writing the numbers we have learned so far.

Let's trace these.

Count the dots on the ladybug and match it to the number:

0

1

2

3

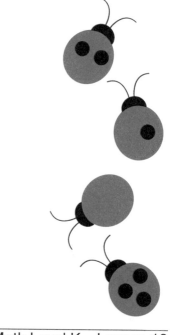

Critical Thinking:

Riddle time!

It is in the house, it is blue, it is not a box. What is it?

Application:

Number of the Week:

3 — T-H-R-E-E spells three.

This is the number 3. Remember how we write a 3, we start near the top:

"Around the tree, around the tree, that's the way we make a 3."

Trace the 3's:

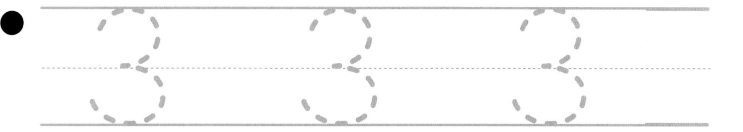

Which one has more? Which one has less?

Critical Thinking:

Using dominoes, play a game of matching the dominoes to see how long of a line you can make.

Application:

Number of the Week:

3 — T-H-R-E-E spells three.

Let's practice our numbers. Try writing the number next to the one you traced.

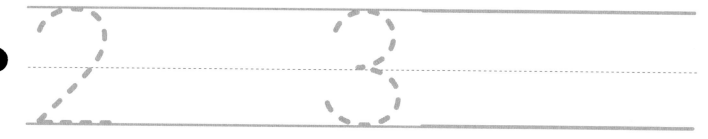

Circle the one that has less in each row.

Critical Thinking:

Color the picture of the fruit stand.

Application:

Number of the Week:

3 — T-H-R-E-E spells three.

This is the number 3. Remember how we write a 3, we start near the top:

"Around the tree, around the tree, that's the way we make a 3."

See if you can trace the three then write two on your own.

Circle the three's:

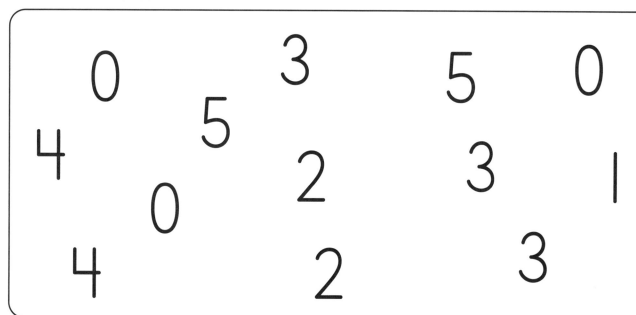

Critical Thinking:

Have students color the picture with the correct answer:

Which image has more items?

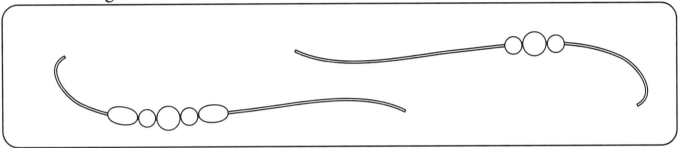

Which image has fewer items?

Which image is almost full?

Which image is almost empty?

Cooking and Measuring, and More or Less

"Mom, Charlie has more blueberries than me!" Charlotte exclaimed. She and Charlie were helping decorate a special cake for the church's 4th of July potluck. "One, two, three, four. . . ." Charlotte carefully counted the berries left in the bowl. There were only 4 berries left.

"I will wash some more blueberries for you to use." Mom reassured. "The cake is looking beautiful, you guys! Great job!"

The twins were carefully lining up blueberries around the top edge of the yummy-looking angel food cake that Mom had made and frosted with real whipped cream. Now Mom was washing and cutting a bowl full of beautiful, bright red strawberries. These would be lined up around the base of the cake, creating a gorgeous red, white, and blue dessert that would taste as good as it looked! The twins couldn't wait to have a big slice of it.

Charlie and Charlotte knew that the colors of the American flag were red, white, and blue. They had each colored a flag coloring page to enter into the coloring competition at the potluck. The winner of that competition would receive a wonderful prize — a red, white, and blue backpack, plus several bunches of helium balloons that were used to decorate the tables. Each of the twins hoped they would win first place.

After the cake was finished and placed in the covered cake plate for safekeeping, the twins ran to get dressed in their patriotic outfits. They each had a pair of new blue denim shorts and a new 4th of July t-shirt. Charlotte especially liked her ponytails today; Mom had tied bright blue, red, and white ribbons at the base of each one!

Later that afternoon, Charlie and Charlotte had fun playing with all of their friends at the potluck. Dad was helping the other men grill massive platters of hamburgers and hot dogs, while Mom helped the other ladies line up the salads, condiments, and desserts. Pastor Donovan was going to be the coloring contest judge after the eating and festivities were finished. The twins were so happy to be part of the celebration for our country's birthday, and the special cake they had helped decorate was delicious!

Calendar:

☐ Complete the calendar.

☐ Review on back of calendar.

Application:

This is an American flag. It is for the country of the United States of America.

What colors do you see on the flag?

| **Teacher** | *If in another country, please use your own country flag for this activity.* |

How many different colors do you see?

How many white stripes do you count?

How many red stripes do you count?

Name______________________________ Exercise 1 Day 66

Critical Thinking:

Sometimes, when we look at a group of items, we can see without counting which group has more and which has less. Without counting, look at the groups below and circle the group with more.

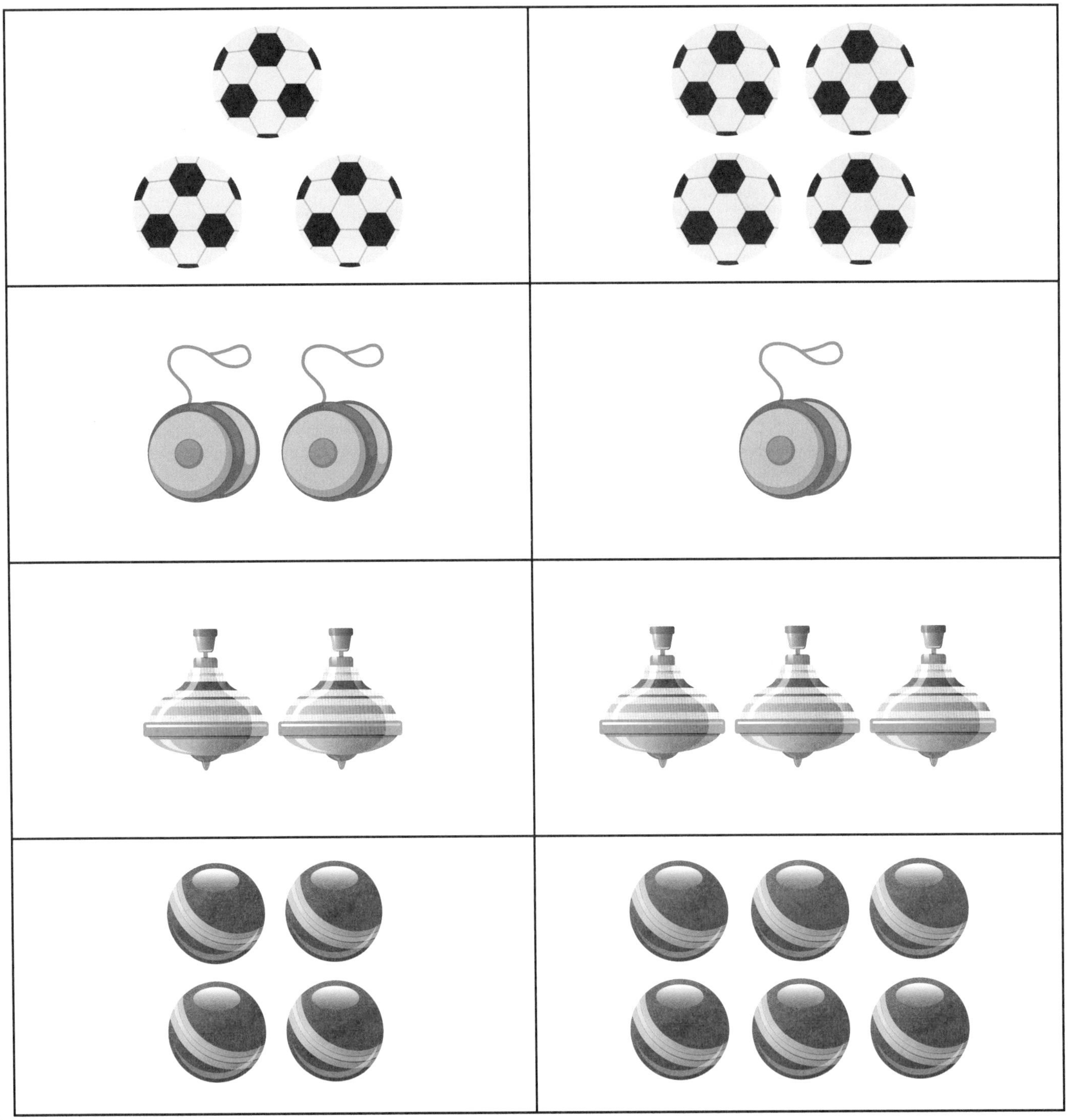

Patriotism is when we love our country. What is something you love about our country?

Application:

Let's measure things!

Teacher

Gather some measuring utensils and have students measure liquids as well as flour or salt.

Critical Thinking:

Without counting, which group has less or fewer than the other?

Application:

Make this favorite family recipe. Don't forget to practice measuring.

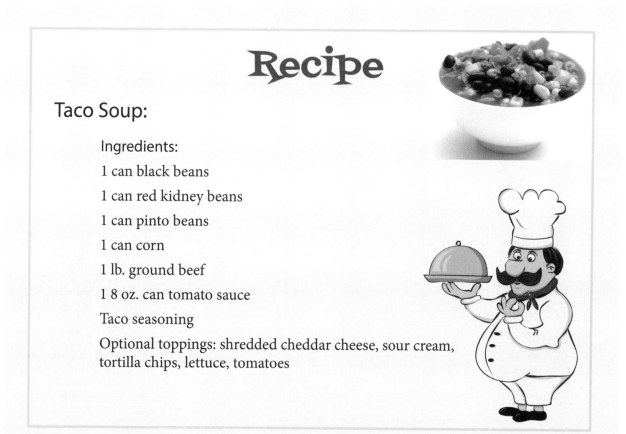

Recipe

Taco Soup:

Ingredients:

1 can black beans

1 can red kidney beans

1 can pinto beans

1 can corn

1 lb. ground beef

1 8 oz. can tomato sauce

Taco seasoning

Optional toppings: shredded cheddar cheese, sour cream, tortilla chips, lettuce, tomatoes

Teacher *The teacher should brown the meat and allow student to help if possible.*

Brown meat in skillet. Use taco seasoning as package states or make your own. Add in all ingredients from cans. Let simmer for 30 minutes or longer (a crockpot works great).

Add toppings as desired, and enjoy!

Critical Thinking:

Match the flags.

Application:

Teacher *Have a 1 cup, 1 tablespoon, and 1 quart measuring container out.*

When cooking, have you noticed that some things hold more than others?

Fill a 1 quart container with water and try to pour all of it into the 1 cup container.

Which one held more? Which one held less water?

Teacher *Continue allowing them to explore this concept.*

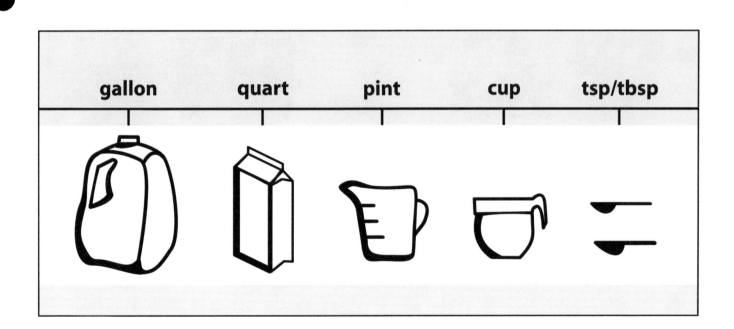

gallon	quart	pint	cup	tsp/tbsp

Critical Thinking:

Mark the box under the container that holds more.

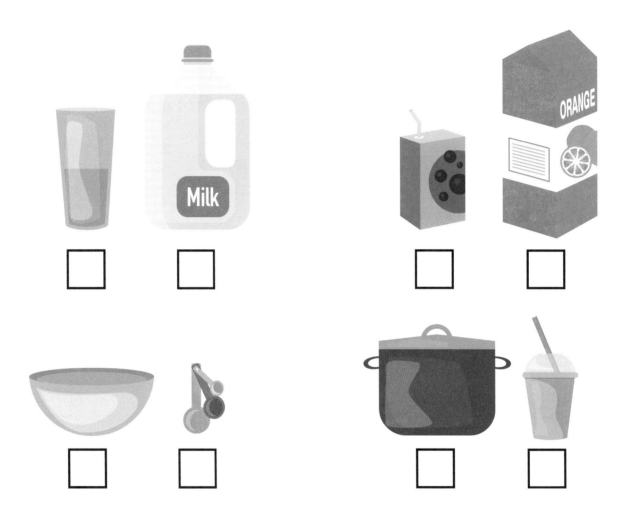

Application:

If we have fewer items on the table than on our plate, then our plate has more. Look at the pile of blocks. Which one has fewer items? Remember, fewer is less than the other.

Now it's your turn. Can you arrange the blocks to show one group with fewer and one group with more? Which group did you make have fewer? Which group has more? How can you tell that this group has more?

Critical Thinking:

Compare the following and place an X on the one that shows more.

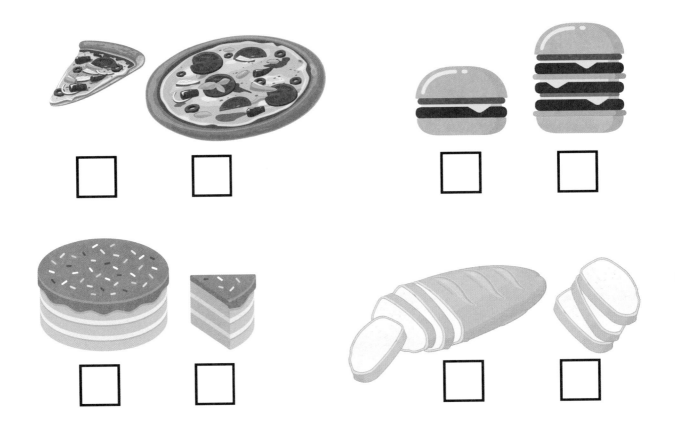

Reviewing Shapes, Matching, and More or Less

"But Dad, I don't wanna take another bath! I just took one last night!" Charlie complained. "Why do I have to wash my hands and take a bath so much?" Charlie sincerely did not like to wash up all the time. He would much rather play, and he honestly did not care if he went to bed dirty.

"Well, kiddo, you have to take a bath because . . . well, for several reasons. The first one is you don't smell too good! You've been outside playing most of the day and you kinda smell like a little, dirty dog!" Dad took a whiff of Charlie's hair and wrinkled his nose like he was smelling a really bad smell. "Ugh!" When Charlie scowled, Dad stopped teasing and said kindly but firmly, "Going to bed dirty is not a good idea, Charlie. Mom works hard to keep our home clean and germ-free. When you take the dirt and germs from outside and put them on the clean sheets that your mama just washed and put on your bed, what do you think happens?"

"I get the sheets all germy?" muttered Charlie.

"Exactly. And when you go to bed dirty without bathing or brushing your teeth, all of those germs just get in there with you and grow. Good hygiene is really important, Charlie," Dad ruffled his son's hair. "I tell you what — after your bath, I'll show you what germs look like. I think after you see them, you won't want to let them grow in your hair, mouth, or bed!"

A little later, Charlie had his eye pressed down on a pocket microscope's eyepiece. "Whoa! Yuck!" Dad had told him and Charlotte that this little microscope magnified objects to make them look 50 times bigger than they really were.

What he was seeing was a patch of dirt that was crusted on the front of the t-shirt he had been wearing all day as he played outside. He could see all kinds of crusty grains of dirt, a few smashed bugs, hairs, and even something that was moving!

"You see, this is why it is so important to take a bath and brush your teeth, especially before going to bed. It's part of taking care of our bodies so we stay as healthy as possible. Our bodies need to be kept clean and well-fed with good nutritious food, and we need to make sure we get enough sleep. Children's bodies grow quickly, so it is especially important for you two to eat and sleep well. When you sleep, your body heals itself and grows a lot. It is truly miraculous."

Calendar:

☐ Complete the calendar.
☐ Review on back of calendar.

Application:

Count how many leaves you have.

Notice how leaves have a stem and a fleshy part. The stem is what connects the leaf to the tree, and then the veins you can see are what help carry the food and water throughout the leaf.

Critical Thinking:

Use the leaves to count how many leaves tall you are.

Count the leaves on each branch.

Application:

Using your leaves, review your basic shapes by making the shapes with leaves: square, circle, triangle, rectangle, oval, and diamond or trace the shapes below.

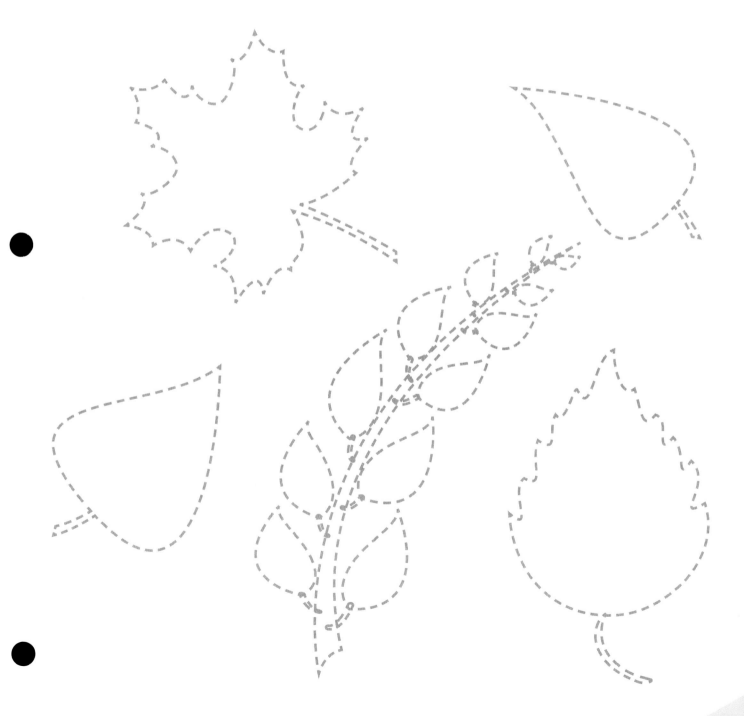

Critical Thinking:

Leaf Matching: Using the leaves you have gathered, sort them to get one of each kind. See if you can use the leaves below to learn what kind it is.

BIRCH   LINDEN   ALDER   OAK

ASPEN   ELM   MAPLE   POPLAR   WILLOW

ROWAN   WALNUT   HAZEL   CHESTNUT   ASH

Application:

Count and match the leaves.

Critical Thinking:

Teacher

Items needed: plain white paper, leaves, tape, and crayons.

Leaf Rubbings:

1. Get plain white paper. (If you have different leaves, it is neat to do different types of leaves and see the differences.)

2. Place a leaf/leaves under it and use painter's tape or other tape to gently secure the edge of the paper (even a clip board would work).

3. Take a crayon or different colored crayons, lay each on its side, and color on the top of the paper back and forth over the leaf to make a leaf rubbing.

4. Can you see the stems of the leaves? Can you see the veins that carry the nutrients the leaf needs?

Application:

Match the leaves and the numbers.

1. chestnut

2. oak

3. elm

4. walnut

5. birch

6. poplar

7. maple

Critical Thinking:

Using the trees below, draw 3 apples on one and 7 apples on the other.

Which tree has more apples? Which tree has fewer apples than the other?

Application:

Which has fewer? Circle the one that has fewer.

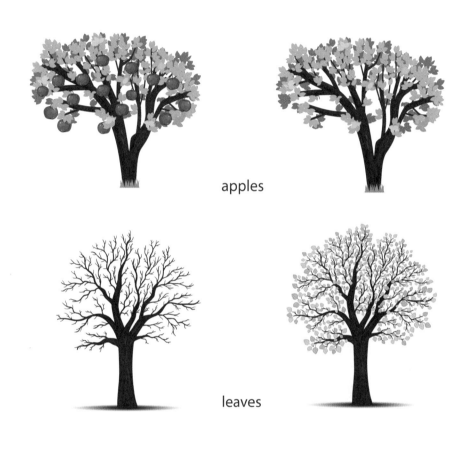

apples

leaves

cones

Critical Thinking:

Match the number leaf to the tree it matches.

Reviewing Counting to 7, and More or Less

"I think my pumpkin is going to win," Charlie grunted as he lifted his "prize-winning" pumpkin onto the van seat before climbing into his seat next to it. "It's the best pumpkin I've ever seen." He patted it carefully. He was certainly proud of the beautiful, orange pumpkin he had grown from a seed all by himself. Charlotte grinned at him.

The family was going to spend the next two days at the county fair, and Charlotte was entering a small wicker basket full of beautiful red, smooth, shiny apples from their one apple tree. Grandma Violet had brought a cutting of one of her prized apple trees to give Mom and Dad after they moved into their own home when they got married, seven years ago. This was the first year that the little tree had produced any fruit, and Charlotte thought that the apples were the prettiest she had ever seen. She was certain her apples would win first prize at the county fair. She had carefully chosen a pretty basket and taken great care to stack as many apples as possible inside of it. She wanted to make sure that the judges got to see the prettiest ones from their tree. Charlotte had also carefully cut up one of the apples and placed it in an airtight container so the judges could taste its delicious, tangy sweetness. She was sure they would enjoy it very much!

Charlie had taken just as much care of his pumpkin. Every day he had gone to the garden to make sure that there were no weeds around it taking nutrients from the soil. He also watched carefully for any type of pesky bug that might want to eat the leaves or burrow into the fruit of his pumpkin. Once, during a thunderstorm that produced some hail, Charlie was certain that his pumpkin would be ruined, but thankfully, there it was, safe and sound and a bright, healthy orange when he ran to check on it afterward. Just this morning, Charlie had measured his pumpkin using Mom's sewing measurement tape. He was so proud to see that it had reached the size it needed to be to enter it into the "large pumpkin division" at the fair. Mom had double-checked for him, and smiled when she saw the measurement of 30 inches. When they set it on the scale, they found out that Charlie's pumpkin weighed in at 12 pounds. It certainly was going to be a fun day at the fair!

Calendar:

☐ Complete the calendar.

☐ Review on back of calendar.

Application:

Count the following items.

How many pumpkins?

How many apples?

Critical Thinking:

Trace and color.

Application:

Count how many pumpkins there are.

Critical Thinking:

Make artwork showing your own pumpkins.

Application:

Draw a line from the pumpkin to the number chart to put the pumpkins in order by number.

‾‾ ‾‾ ‾‾ ‾‾ ‾‾
1   2   3   4   5

Critical Thinking:

Draw a line from the apples to fill the baskets with the correct amount.

Name_____

Application:

Have you ever wondered what the inside of a pumpkin looked like?

It's full of seeds! Color one seed blue, two seeds red, three seeds yellow, four seeds green, and five seeds orange.

Critical Thinking:

Teacher

Materials needed today: crayons, a nickel, a dime, and a quarter with a piece of plain white paper.

Take your paper and lay it over the coins. Now rub your crayon over each one to create an image on the paper. Which image is the smallest? Which image is the biggest? Which image is in between the smallest and the biggest?

Application:

Charlie and Charlotte gathered their pumpkins and apples. Did they have more pumpkins or apples? How many do they have of each?

Critical Thinking:

Color the farmer's field full of pumpkins. How many pumpkins did you color?

Basic Sequencing, and Counting Review

Mom poked her head around the doorway of the twins' room. Charlie and Charlotte were playing with their barnyard set, which was spread out over most of the space between their beds. "I told you two to pick up your toys! Please listen and obey. Charlotte, you pick up all of the animals and put them away while Charlie brushes his teeth, then he can finish cleaning up the other toys while you brush your teeth. Come along now, Charlie!"

Charlie grumbled as he made his way down the hall to the bathroom. He and Charlotte had been having a hard time remembering the sequence of preparing for bed, so Mom had created a chart to hang on their bedroom wall. At the top of the chart was the title, "1, 2, 3 . . . Get ready for bed!" Next to the number 1, there was a picture of a bathtub, next to the number 2 was a picture of pajamas, next to the number 3 was a picture of a toothbrush and tube of toothpaste.

The twins were good at numbers 1 and 2, but they almost always got distracted by their toys after that. Mom was teaching them to stay on task and finish the process of preparing for bed.

As Charlotte picked up the toy animals and put them in their box, she thought about how everything in life was done in steps. She had watched her mom bake and cook, and she knew that it was important to understand how to follow the sequence of instructions.

When Charlie returned to the bedroom, he flashed Charlotte a smile to show his clean, white teeth. "My teeth are so clean they squeak!" he said, rubbing his fingertip over his front two teeth. Charlotte giggled and skipped down the hall to the bathroom to brush her teeth.

A few minutes later, Mom and Dad came into the children's bedroom to say prayers and kiss them goodnight. As the twins snuggled down into their pillows and pulled their covers over their shoulders, the peaceful sounds of the evening drifted through their open window.

Calendar:

☐ Complete the calendar.

☐ Review on back of calendar.

Application:

Sequence means the order in which things go or happen. Think of a chicken. It starts as an egg, hatches to become a chick, and then grows into a chicken.

Look at the example below.

Point to which one would happen first, before the others.

Which one would be next?

Which one would be the last one?

In order to make our sequence be in the right order, we need to draw an egg first, then a chick, and last a chicken.

Draw the correct sequence below:

Critical Thinking:

Look at the pictures. Place number 1 on what happened first in this sequence, then a 2 for what happened next in the sequence. Write a 3 for what happened last in the sequence.

Application:

Remember, *sequence* means the order in which things happen.

Let's look at this sequence for bedtime and you put it in order of first, middle, and last.

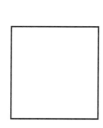 

Critical Thinking:

Create 3 different parts of a sequence of building a house with blocks.

> **Teacher**
>
> *The teacher will need to help them understand that we need to see the beginning, middle, and end of them building a house with blocks. Step 1 might be one block. Step 2 might be halfway built. Step 3 would be a completed house.*

If you were going to begin to build a house with blocks, what would you begin with? Start doing that now.

Application:

Do you remember what a *sequence* is? Yes, it's means the order in which things go or happen.

Put this sequence in order.

Critical Thinking:

A sequence can also happen with numbers. Like in a phone number or even when counting.

Put the correct number in the blank by seeing which numbers are missing in the sequence: 1, 2, 3, 4.

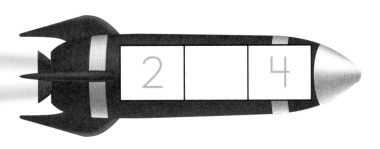

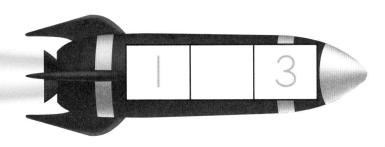

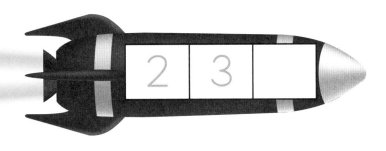

Application:

Count the pizza circles first, then sequence.

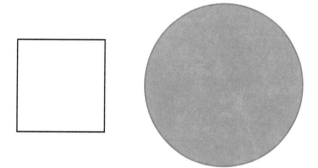

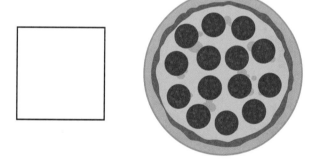

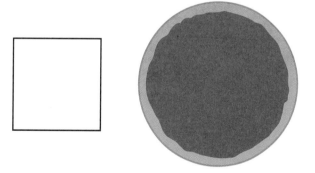

Critical Thinking

Have your teacher tell you the nursery rhyme "Humpty Dumpty" and listen for the beginning, middle, and end. Retell the sequence of story events, then color the image below.

Application:

Color these objects that are in sequence.

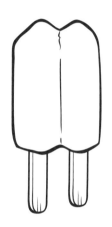  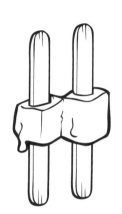 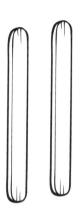

Critical Thinking:

Look at the pictures. Place number 1 on what happened first in this sequence, then a 2 for what happened next in the sequence. Write a 3 for what happened last in the sequence.

Completing the Sequence, and Number Review to 3

"So, kids, if your clothes are ever on fire, what do you do?" asked Fireman George.

"Stop, drop, and roll!!" the children shouted together.

"Yes! You are correct. We just need to be cautious. Fire is not something we play with, right?" The kind fireman laid his hand on Charlie's head. A large group of kindergarten-age students from four churches in the area had come in for a tour of the firehouse. Fireman George did not want to make the children afraid, but he also wanted them to understand how we should all have a healthy respect for fire.

"Fireman George, can we see inside the firetruck?" Charlie asked.

"Yes! Can we?" several other children echoed the question.

"Yes! In fact, if it's okay with your parents and group leaders, you can all have a ride in the truck," Fireman George answered. After a few instructions on what to do inside the firetruck, the fireman divided the group into smaller groups of ten. He helped the first group into the truck and made sure that they were all seated before climbing up into the driver's seat of the truck.

Later that afternoon, Charlie and Charlotte sat at the kitchen table chatting about their exciting trip to the firehouse. They had been so surprised at how huge the firetruck was and how high up in the air they felt when they had their turn to take a ride in it. It felt like they were in a tall building looking down at all of their friends who were lined up waiting for their turn.

"I'm sure glad that Fireman George taught us what to do if our clothes catch on fire, but I really hope that never happens!" Charlotte shuddered.

"Yeah. But it's really good to know how to be safe and to know that we shouldn't play with fire," added Charlie. Both of the twins were happy to be home where they felt safe. They knew that their parents would always be careful and take good care of them.

Calendar:

☐ Complete the calendar.

☐ Review on back of calendar.

Application:

Look at the pictures. Place number 1 on what happened first in this sequence, then a 2 for what happened next in the sequence. Write a 3 for what happened last in the sequence.

Critical Thinking:

Reviewing numbers 1–3.

Remember, this is the number 1. We would write it by: straight down, then you're done. That's the way we make a 1. Trace this now with your finger.

This is a number 2. We would write it by: over, around and back on the track, that's the way we write a 2. Trace this now.

This is a number 3. We would write it by: around the tree, around the tree, that's the way we make a 3. Trace it now.

These are the numbers we will be using to show steps. Let's repeat these numbers and trace them one more time.

Remember, if your clothing or a part of you catches on fire, here are the steps you would take to put out the fire.

     1. STOP   2. DROP   3. ROLL

Application:

Trace and count. Color the squares for the amount of each number.

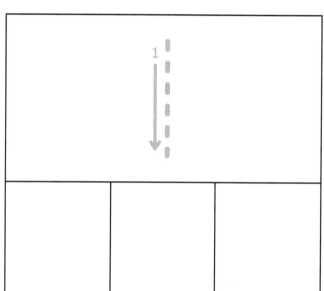

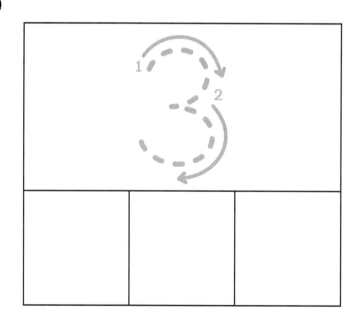

Critical Thinking:

Let's practice our steps again of what to do if you or your clothing catch on fire.

1. STOP
2. DROP
3. ROLL

Practice this again by role playing.

Stop   Drop   Roll

Application:

Trace and count. Color the squares for the amount of each number.

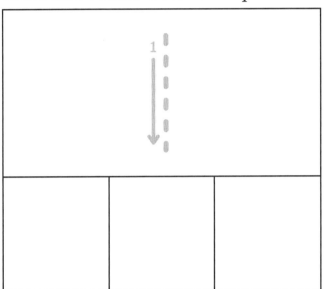

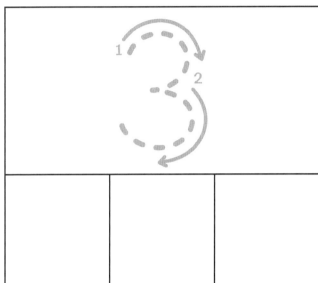

Critical Thinking:

Let's practice our steps again of what to do if you or your clothing catch on fire.

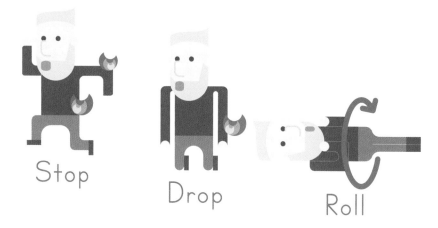

Stop   Drop   Roll

Another time we use numbers in a special order is if we have an emergency. We dial 9-1-1.

We NEVER call 911 for fun. If we do that, then the people talking to you cannot help someone with a real emergency.

Use this diagram to practice dialing 911.

Application:

Trace, color the amount, and circle the numbers.

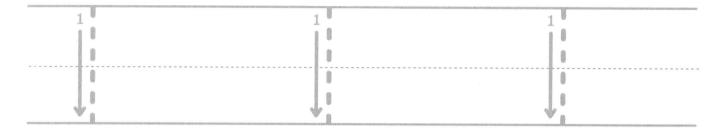

● Color 1.

Circle the one's.

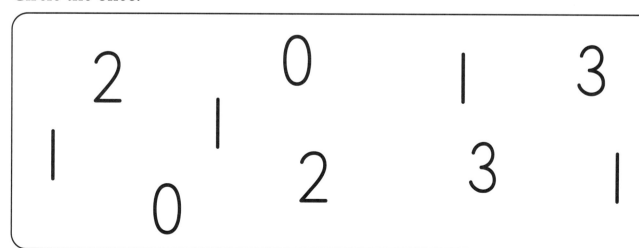

Critical Thinking:

Review Stop, Drop, and Roll

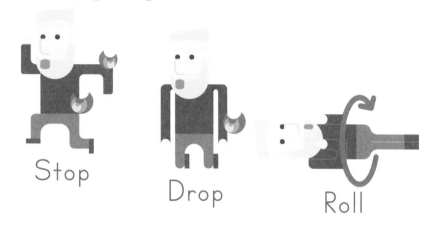

Stop   Drop   Roll

911

We NEVER call 911 for fun. If we do that, then the people talking to you cannot help someone with a real emergency.

Use this diagram to practice dialing 911.

Using blocks and a die, roll the die and build that amount of a tower.

Application:

Trace, color the amount, and circle the numbers.

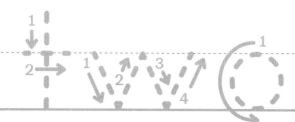

Color 2.

Circle the two's.

2	0	l	3
l			3
	l		
0	2	3	2

Critical Thinking:

Review Stop, Drop, and Roll and dialing 911.

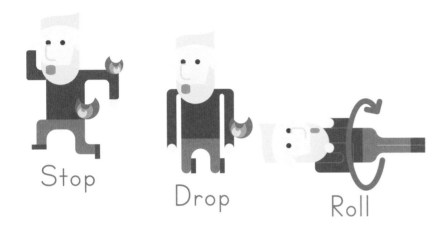

Stop

Drop

Roll

Connect dominoes to make the longest train you can. Draw your domino train in the space below.

Lesson **19**

"Four is my favorite number!" declared Charlotte as she carefully folded the last napkin and placed it on the table to the left of Dad's dinner plate. "That's because there are four of us in our family!"

The children had helped Mom make a special supper in honor of Dad's birthday. They had helped scrub four red potatoes so Mom could put them in the oven to bake, and they had helped decorate the cake that she had made for dessert. There were balloons in the center of the table and handmade cards from the twins carefully arranged by Dad's plate. The house smelled so delicious that it was making Charlie's tummy growl!

"He's home! Daddy's home!" Charlotte shouted from her spot by the front window as her father pulled his work truck into the driveway and parked in front of the garage. She ran to the side door and opened it for him with a shout of, "Happy birthday, Daddy!"

"Why, thank you, Charlotte!" Dad scooped her up and squeezed her. His chin was bristly and rough, but Charlotte didn't care. She loved the smell of her daddy; he smelled like fresh air and wood chips.

"We made you something special, Daddy," Charlotte exclaimed, wiggling to get down. Grabbing her father's hand, she pulled him around the corner and into the kitchen, where Mom was taking the baked potatoes out of the oven and placing them on a plate.

"Look! This is for you, Dad!" Charlotte and Charlie shouted together in excitement, pointing to the yummy birthday cake in the middle of the table. "And we made you these cards all by ourselves!" Charlie added.

"Wow, kids, this is so wonderful! Thank you!" Dad ruffled both of the kids' hair before turning to his wife. "Do I have time to take a quick shower, Honey?" he asked.

"Sure, I still have to thicken this gravy," she answered. She had made her husband's favorite meal: cheesy meatloaf and gravy, baked potatoes, coconut-parmesan broccoli, and for dessert, a vanilla cake with creamy buttercream frosting.

"One, two, three, aaaand . . . four!" Charlotte counted as she carefully placed the baked potatoes on each of the plates. "One, two, three, aaaand four!" she counted again as she placed a glass in front of each place setting. Four was a good number; it meant that her whole family was here for this special dinner.

Calendar:

☐ Complete the calendar.

☐ Review on back of calendar.

Application:

Number of the Week: 4 — F-O-U-R spells four.

This is the number 4. Count the 4 daisies.

When we write a 4, we start at the top:

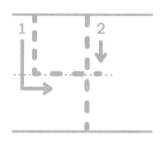

"Down and over, then down again, that's the way we make a 4."

Trace the 4's:

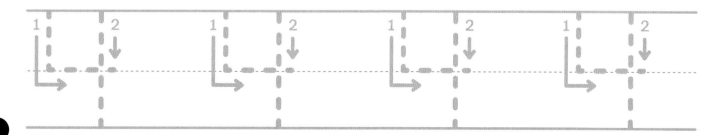

Critical Thinking:

Shape Review: Color the shapes the color stated below, and then count how many there are.

Color the circles red. There are _____ circles.

Color the squares blue. There are _____ squares.

Color the rectangles orange. There are _____ rectangles.

Color the triangles brown. There are _____ triangles.

Color the stars yellow. There are _____ stars.

Color the diamonds green. There are _____ diamonds.

Teacher *Have students count. Teacher can write in the correct number.*

Application:

Number of the Week:

4 — F-O-U-R spells four.

This is the number 4. When we write a 4, we start at the top:

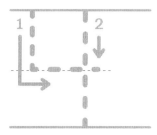

"Down and over, then down again, that's the way we make a 4."

Trace the 4's:

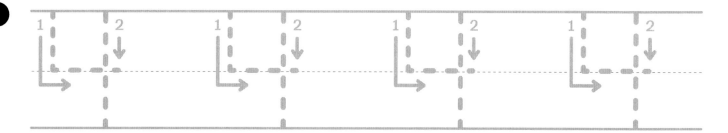

Color the number 4.

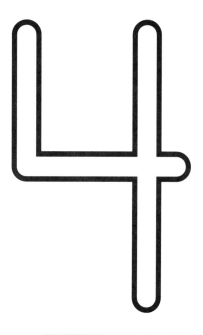

Critical Thinking:

Shape Review:

Make the shape of a person by tracing the shapes below:

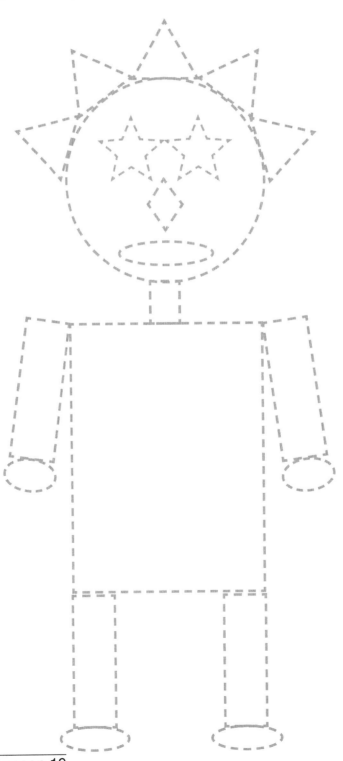

Application:

Number of the Week:

4 — F-O-U-R spells four.

Let's practice writing the numbers we have learned so far.

Let's trace these.

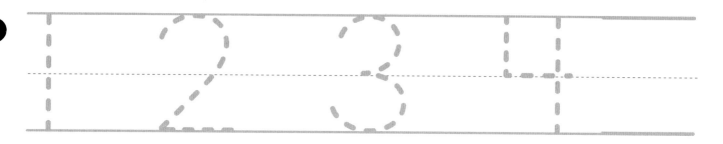

Teacher

Hide and Seek 4's Game:

Hide 4s written on post-it notes/index cards around the room. Have them find all the 4s and hop each time they find one.

Critical Thinking:

Match the other half of the shape.

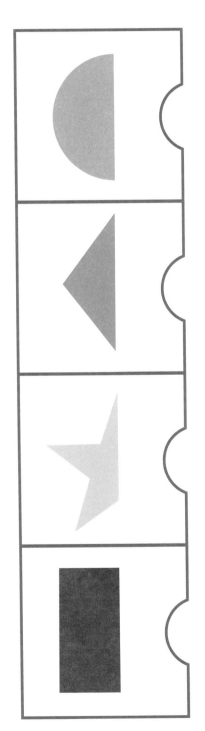
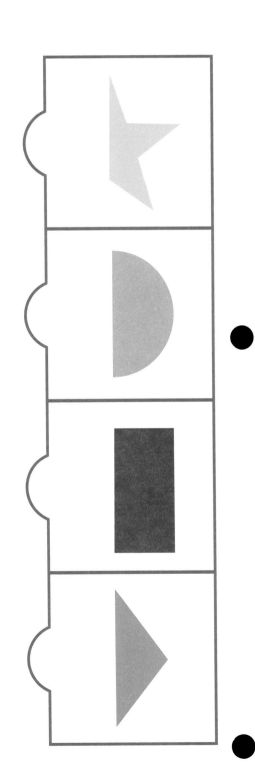

Application:

Number of the Week:
4 — F-O-U-R spells four.

Let's practice our numbers. Try writing the number next to the one you traced.

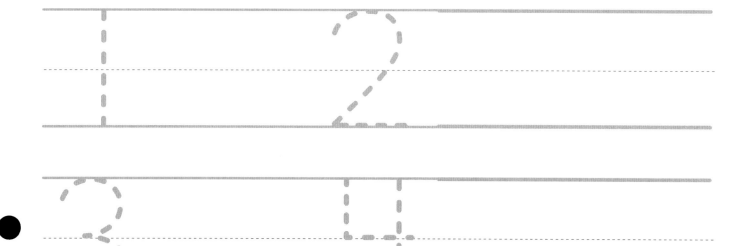

Use painter's tape or post-it notes (or sidewalk chalk outside) to make a number line from 0–5. Hop from 0–5 as you count.

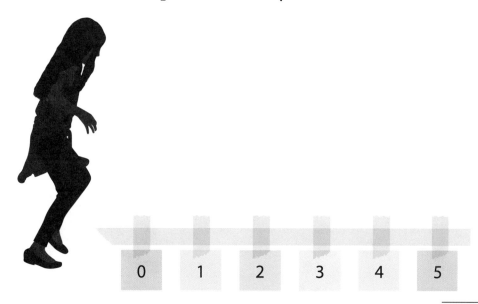

| 0 | 1 | 2 | 3 | 4 | 5 |

Critical Thinking:

There are 4 objects here. Which one is the biggest? Which one is teeny tiny? Which one do you think would weigh the most?

Application:

Number of the Week:

4 — F-O-U-R spells four.

This is the number 4. When we write a 4, we start at the top:

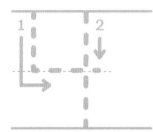

"Down and over, then down again, that's the way we make a 4."

See if you can trace the four then write two on your own.

Circle all the number 4's.

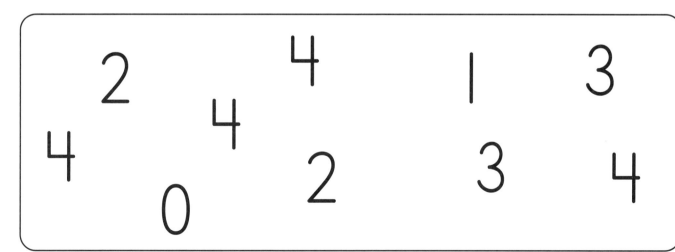

Critical Thinking:

Match the shapes below with their name. Your teacher can read the words for you.

square

oval

triangle

circle

heart

star

rectangle

"You are doing a great job with learning to tie your shoes! I'm so proud of your determination," Mom encouraged Charlie.

"Thanks, Mom," Charlie was concentrating so hard on the steps of tying his sneakers that his tongue was sticking out of the corner of his mouth — something he did when he was thinking hard about something.

"Like this, Mama?" Charlotte jumped to her feet, with both shoes tied. She had learned how to tie her shoes a few weeks ago, but had been practicing along with Charlie. She was proud of her accomplishment and of her brother's determination. "Good job, Charlie!" she exclaimed when she saw that he had moved on to his second shoe lace.

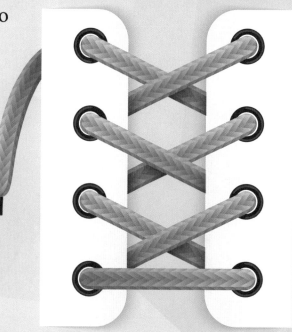

"Thanks," Charlie smiled, "you did good, too, Charlotte. There! I did it!" he proclaimed, standing to his feet. He looked down at his shoes. He really was very proud of this huge accomplishment. His shoes had 5 eyelets on either side. He had carefully counted them when he laced up his shoes. Charlotte's shoe only had 4 eyelets on either side, so hers were a little easier to lace up than his.

Both twins had learned that lacing and tying shoes was a sequence of steps that you had to be careful to follow.

If you did something out of order, it didn't work out so well. Mom had shown them both how to make the laces in each shoe nice and even before crisscrossing them and feeding them through the eyelets. Charlie liked how he could pull on the laces to tighten his shoes. Dad had told him last night that being able to tie his shoes was a big step in growing up.

Calendar:

☐ Complete the calendar.
☐ Review on back of calendar.

Application:

Number of the Week:

5 — F-I-V-E spells five.

This is the number 5. Count the 5 flamingos.

When we write a 5, we start at the top:

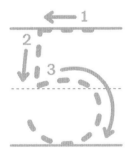

"Make a hat (across at the top line) then a neck (down from top to midline) and a round belly."

Trace the 5's:

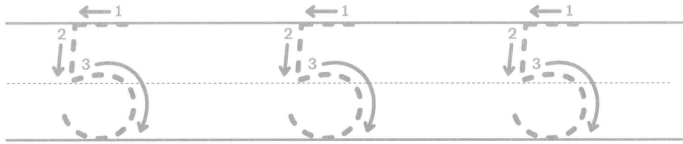

Critical Thinking:

Dot-to-Dot Fun: Connect the dots from 1–5.

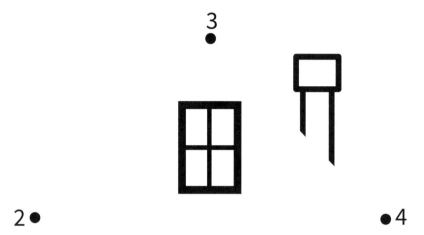

Application:

Number of the Week:

5 — F-I-V-E spells five.

This is the number 5. When we write a 5, we start at the top:

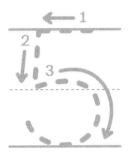

"Make a hat (across at the top line) then a neck (down from top to midline) and a round belly."

Trace the 5's:

Creative Thinking:

Color the number 5.

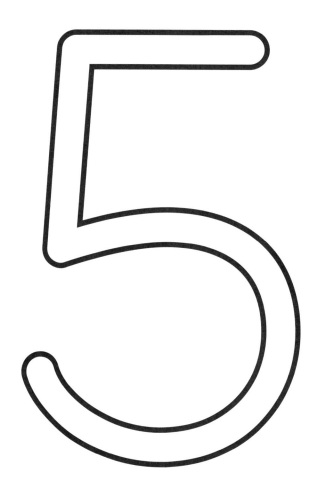

Application:

Number of the Week:

5 — F-I-V-E spells five.

Let's practice writing some of the numbers we have learned so far.

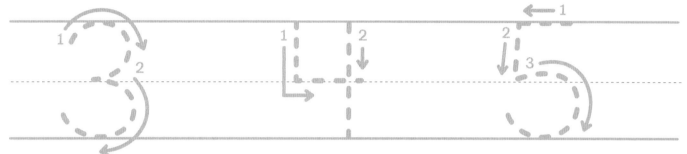

Let's trace these.

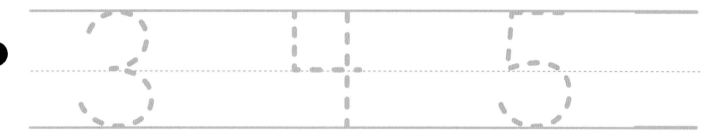

Do you remember how many eyelets were on Charlie's shoes? Right, 5. Count to 5. Practice tying your shoes.

Circle 5 buttons.

Name______________________________

Critical Thinking:

In the boxes on the right, place these numbers in the correct order.

5

1

0

2

4

3

Name_____

Application:

Number of the Week:

5 — F-I-V-E spells five.

Let's practice our numbers. Try writing the number next to the one you traced.

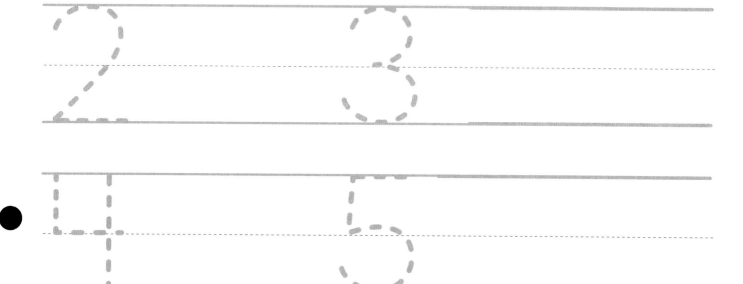

Count to 5. Count the 5 objects by touching each one.

Critical Thinking:

Roll and build.

Roll the die and build a tower of that many blocks.

Teacher *Materials needed: a die and blocks.*

Application:

Number of the Week:

5 — F-I-V-E spells five.

This is the number 5. When we write a 5, we start at the top:

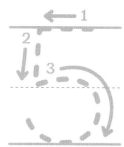

"Make a hat (across at the top line) then a neck (down from top to midline) and a round belly." See if you can trace the five then write two on your own.

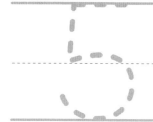

Color 5 buttons.

Critical Thinking:

Connect the dots from 1–5. What did you make? Color it if you'd like.

"Mama, when are Grandma and Grandpa coming?" Charlie stopped at the front window to peer out at the driveway for what seemed the hundredth time that morning. The twins were so excited for their grandparents' visit. They had been spending the morning helping Mom clean and prepare for their coming.

"Grandma just texted and said that they were about a half an hour away, Charlie," Mom answered. "Could you and Charlotte please finish dusting the end tables while I finish sweeping the porch?"

"Yes, Mama," Charlotte answered for both of them. "Here, Charlie, you do that end table, and I'll do this one. I'll have to clean up these cookie crumbs first." Charlotte loved to clean, and she often took over the job, instructing her brother to do this or that. Charlie didn't mind. He didn't like cleaning as much as Charlotte, but he did want to help prepare for his grandparents' coming. They were going to stay for a week, and Charlie was looking forward to the yummy feast he knew his mom and grandma would be preparing for the family.

Charlotte was excited! Mom had given her permission to set and decorate the table for dinner. She was going to set 6 plates, 6 sets of silverware, 6 drinking glasses, and 6 napkins, which she was going to place in the pretty, brass napkin ring. She knew that she needed 6 place settings because she needed one for each of the 6 family members. She

was also going to make a beautiful centerpiece using candles, colored leaves, and the little, clay bowls that she and Charlie had made in arts and crafts class at church the week before.

As a finishing touch, they were going to hang a "Thankful Tree" on the wall in the dining room. They always put it up around special days. Last week, Mom had helped them cut out the trunk of the tree, using brown paper, and each day for the last week they had each hung a leaf with something they were thankful for written on it. Both of the children had hung 6 leaves on the tree — one for Sunday, one for Monday, one for Tuesday, one for Wednesday, one for Thursday, and one for Friday. Today was Saturday and they were anxious to hang up more.

Calendar:

☐ Complete the calendar.

☐ Review on back of calendar.

Application:

Number of the Week:

6 — S-I-X spells six.

This is the number 6. Count the 6 flowers.

When we write a 6, we start at the top:

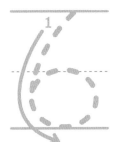

"Make a hoop and then a loop, that's the way to make a 6."

Trace the 6's:

Critical Thinking:

Count the shapes below.

Count to 6 as you clap.

Circle the 6's.

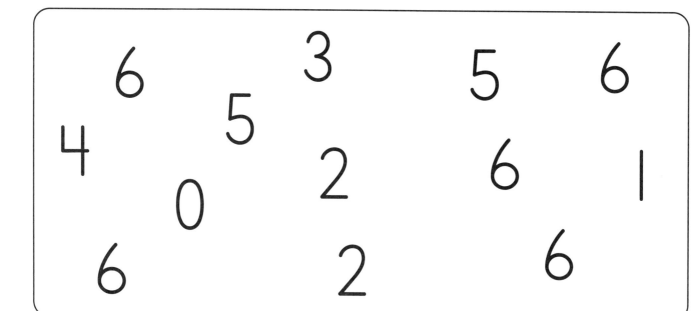

Application:

Number of the Week:

6 — S-I-X spells six.

This is the number 6. When we write a 6, we start at the top:

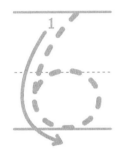

"Make a hoop and then a loop, that's the way to make a 6."

Trace the 6's:

Count and circle 6 objects in each row.

Critical Thinking:

Color the number 6.

Application:

Number of the Week:

6 — S-I-X spells six. Let's practice writing the numbers we have learned so far.

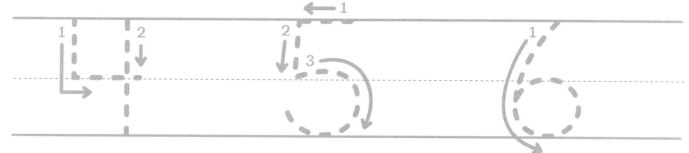

Let's trace these.

Color 6 lambs.

Critical Thinking:

Find 6 differences.

Application:

Number of the Week:

6 — S-I-X spells six.

Let's practice writing some of the numbers we have learned so far.

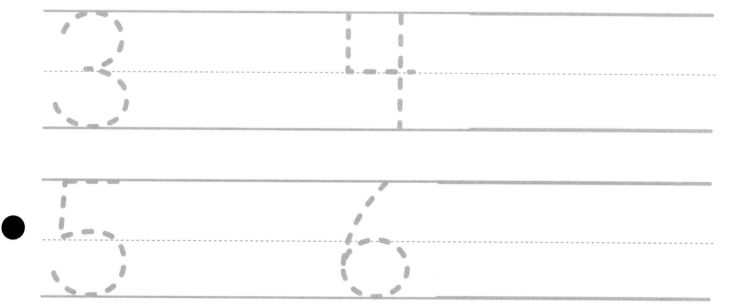

Which group has 6? Circle it.

Critical Thinking:

Color by number.

Application:

Number of the Week:

6 — S-I-X spells six.

This is the number 6. When we write a 6, we start at the top:

"Make a hoop and then a loop, that's the way to make a 6."

See if you can trace the six then write two more on your own.

Critical Thinking:

Number Maze.

Complete the maze to help the 6 bees find their way back to the hive.

Number of the Week: 7, Counting, and Comparisons

"Number 1, my family. Number 2, my home. Number 3, my clothes. Number 4, my toys. Number 5, my friends. Number 6, food! Number 7, that I can run and play and talk and think!" Charlotte pointed at each of her brightly colored "Thankful Tree" leaves as she told her family what was written or drawn on each one. Her family clapped and cheered, and Charlotte bowed and smiled.

"Mama, I have an idea!" Charlotte's words brought a pause to the adult conversation.

"What is it, Honey?" her mom responded, while reaching over to brush her daughter's hair back out of her face.

"What if Charlie and I made a thankful project for each day of the week? There are 7 days, right?" Mama nodded and Charlotte continued, "We could create a poster of all the things that happen in that day that we are thankful for! At the end of the week, we would have 7 posters — one for each day!"

"That's a wonderful idea, Charlotte!" Grandpa's eyes twinkled as he smiled at his granddaughter. Mom and Dad smiled and nodded their heads in agreement. Charlie and Charlotte looked at each other and cheered. They loved making posters, and this project sounded like so much fun!

"You know, children," Grandma Violet's voice brought the chatter around the table to quiet. "This thankful poster project reminds me of a verse in the Bible. It's a verse about remembering the good things that the Lord has done for us." Grandma turned to Grandpa, "Grandpa, would you read us that Scripture?"

"Yes, Dear," Grandpa flipped the pages of the family Bible to Joshua 4 and read the story of how God instructed His special people to set up stones of remembrance so that the future generations and all of the world would know the mighty and good deeds of God and fear Him forever.

Calendar:

☐ Complete the calendar.
☐ Review on back of calendar.

Name_____

Exercise **1** Day 106

Application:

Number of the Week:

7 — S-E-V-E-N spells seven.

This is the number 7. Count the 7 bugs.

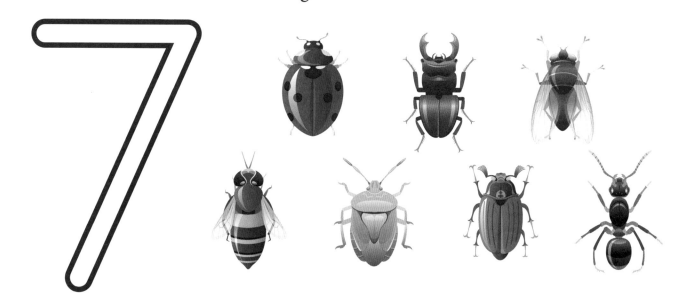

When we write a 7, we start at the top line:

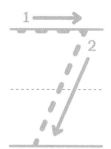

"Go across the sky and down from heaven, that's the way to make a 7."

Trace the 7's:

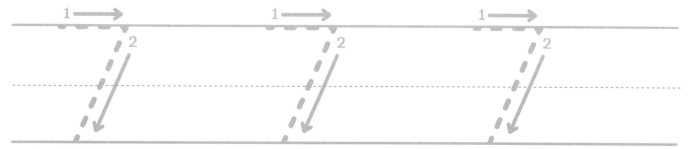

Math Level K – Lesson 22   261

Critical Thinking:

Help the 7 find the correct bundle of apples by tracing the right path.

Application:

Number of the Week:

7 — S-E-V-E-N spells seven.

This is the number 7. When we write a 7, we start at the top line:

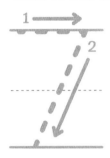

"Go across the sky and down from heaven, that's the way to make a 7."

Trace the 7's:

Count to 7 as you jump over a rope (or jump rope) or hop.

Critical Thinking:

Circle the carton with 7 eggs.

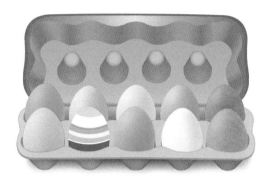

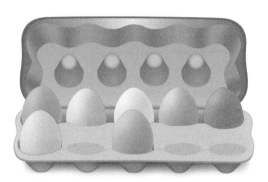

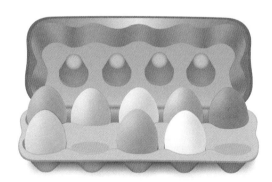

Application:

Number of the Week:

7 — S-E-V-E-N spells seven.

Let's practice writing the numbers we have learned so far.

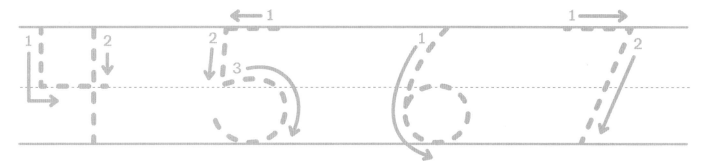

Let's trace these.

Count out 7 blocks and stack them.

Critical Thinking:

Number Maze.

Complete the maze to help the gardener water the 7 flowers.

Application:

Number of the Week:

7 — S-E-V-E-N spells seven.

Let's practice our numbers. Try writing the number next to the one you traced.

Color the number 7.

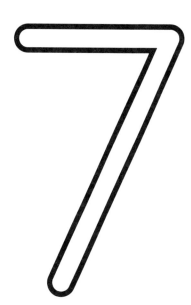

Critical Thinking:

Follow the instruction to make towers using your blocks:

Teacher *Student will need blocks for this activity.*

Tower 1 has 10 blocks. Make that now.

Tower 2 has 7 blocks. Make that now.

Tower 3 has 4 blocks. Make that now.

Which tower is the tallest?

Which tower is the shortest?

Which tower has the most blocks?

Which tower has the least blocks?

Application:

Number of the Week:

7 — S-E-V-E-N spells seven.

This is the number 7. When we write a 7, we start at the top line:

"Go across the sky and down from heaven, that's the way to make a 7."

See if you can trace the seven then write two more on your own:

Circle the 7's.

7   3   7   6

5

4   2   7   1

0

7   2   6

Critical Thinking:

Circle the number that is larger or more than the other numbers:

2   5   7   3

Connect the dots from 1–7. Once done, you may color it.

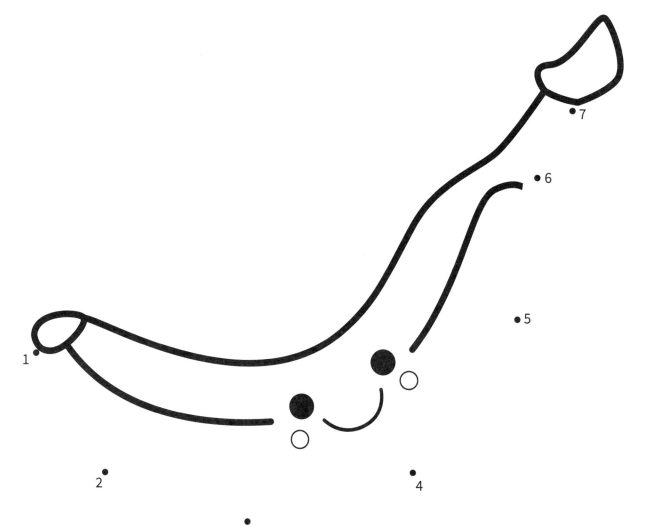

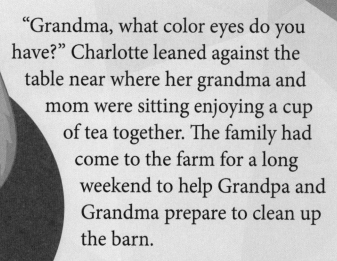

"Grandma, what color eyes do you have?" Charlotte leaned against the table near where her grandma and mom were sitting enjoying a cup of tea together. The family had come to the farm for a long weekend to help Grandpa and Grandma prepare to clean up the barn.

"My eyes are green-hazel, Honey," Grandma smiled at her granddaughter. "Why do you ask, Charlotte?"

"Charlie and I are making a graph showing the color of everyone's eyes," Charlotte explained, showing Grandma her paper. "Mom says that graphing is a way of measuring things." Charlotte brushed her hair back out of her eyes. She felt very important; learning to graph and measure things was a very grown-up project. "So far, I have Grandpa's, Daddy's, mine, and Charlie's. See?"

"That's very nice, Charlotte," Grandma smiled at the little girl. "What color did you put down for Grandpa's eyes?"

"Brown," Charlotte answered, pointing to Grandpa's eye-color on the graph. "See? His are the only brown ones in the family! I didn't know that. Mama, what color are your eyes?" Charlotte moved closer to her mom and peered into her eyes. "Hmmm . . . I think they are blue . . . or grey? What color should I put, Mom?"

"Blue," Mom smiled. "Sometimes my eyes look grey — like today, because I'm wearing a grey sweatshirt, see?" Charlotte nodded. She didn't know that eyes could change colors! This could be very hard to show on her graph. "Charlotte, yours and Charlie's eyes look grey sometimes, too. Did you know that? And Dad's, which are green-hazel like Grandma's, sometimes look very green."

"I think I better just write what they usually are," Charlotte thought for a moment. "Otherwise, I will have to change my graph and make it much bigger!"

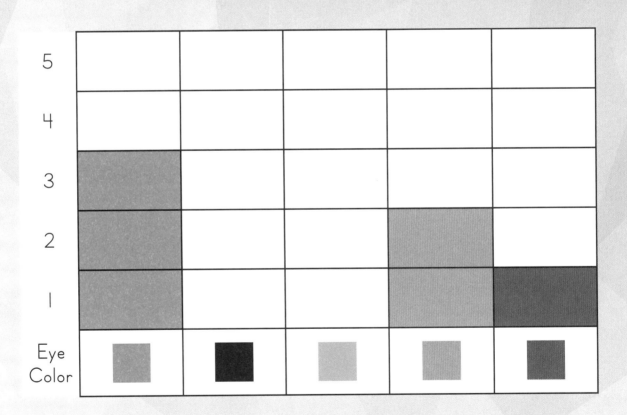

Calendar:

☐ Complete the calendar.
☐ Review on back of calendar.

Application:

Number of the Week:

8 — E-I-G-H-T spells eight.

This is the number 8. Count the 8 crayons.

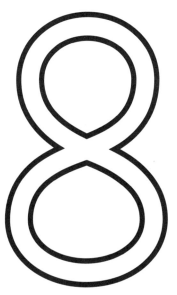 

When we write an 8, we start at the top line:

"Make an S, do not wait, go back up and close the gate."

Trace the 8's:

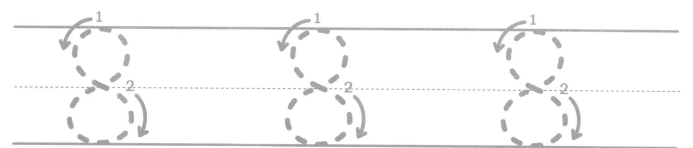

Critical Thinking:

Remember that a *graph* is a picture that tells us how much or how many of different kinds of things. It is a way we can measure. An example would be how many dogs and cats are at an animal shelter. Here is an example.

Notice that *one side has numbers* for how many, and *the other side tells what* we are *measuring or counting*. You can count the squares to see how many there are. The taller the squares or bar means the more there are.

How many dogs are at the shelter?

How many cats are at the shelter?

> **Teacher**
> *Use post-it notes to create a graph on the wall or floor. Label some with each eye color and then have them draw a picture of each family member on a different post-it. They will then place their drawing of each family member in the correct eye color spot to create a graph.*

Now we will create a graph using eye color and our family.

How many people have blue eyes?

How many have brown eyes?

How many have green eyes?

How many have hazel eyes?

Do you know which color has the most?

Application:

Number of the Week:

8 — E-I-G-H-T spells eight.

This is the number 8. When we write an 8, we start at the top line:

"Make an S, do not wait, go back up and close the gate."

Trace the 8's:

Critical Thinking:

Let's graph all of your shoes (up to 8). We will graph them by color. Use the graph below to fill in (you might do one as a multi-color).

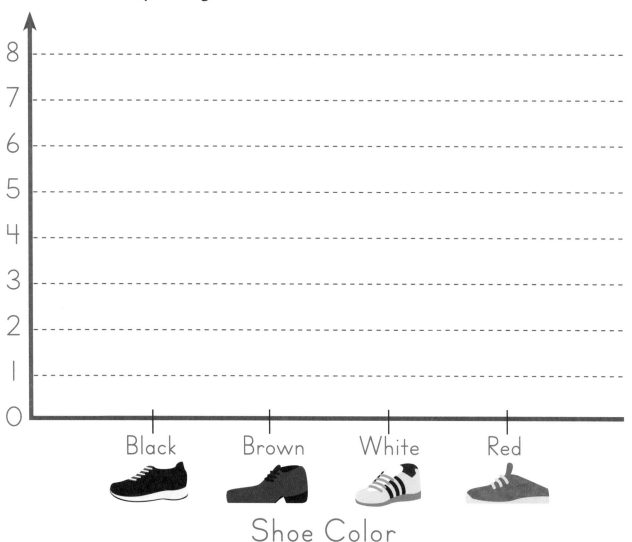

How many colors did we have? Which color had the most?

Application:

Number of the Week:

8 — E-I-G-H-T spells eight.

Let's practice writing the numbers we have learned so far.

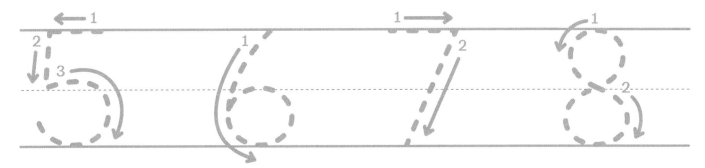

Let's trace these.

Color the number 8.

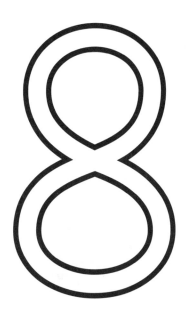

Critical Thinking:

Help the 8 find her correct pitcher of daffodils by tracing the right path.

Name________________________________

Application:

Number of the Week:

8 — E-I-G-H-T spells eight. Let's practice our numbers. Try writing the number next to the one you traced.

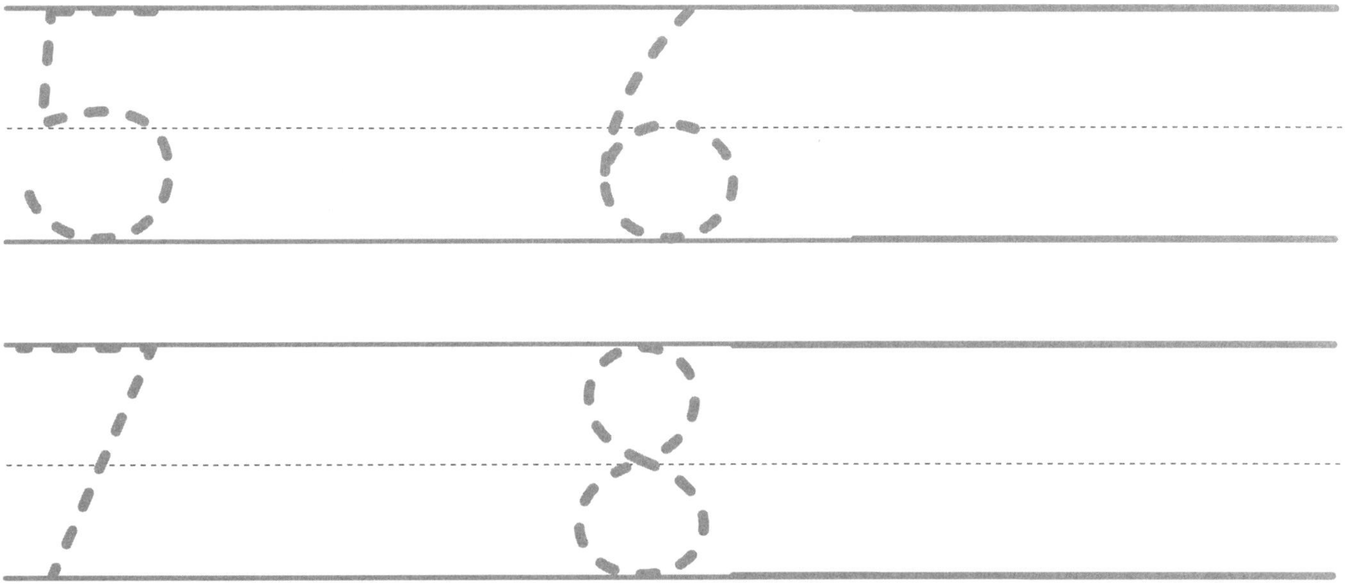

Circle the 8's.

8 3 7 6

4 5 2 8 1

0

8 2 8

Creative Thinking:

Today we will be reading a graph.

Look at this graph below and answer the questions.

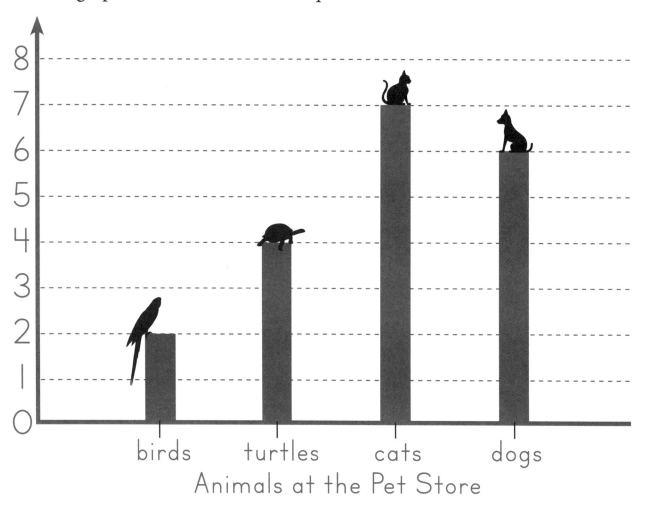

Animals at the Pet Store

How many birds are at the pet store?

How many turtles are at the pet store?

How many cats are at the pet store?

How many dogs are at the pet store?

You did an awesome job today on counting the animals in the graph!

Application:

Number of the Week:

8 — E-I-G-H-T spells eight.

This is the number 8. When we write an 8, we start at the top line:

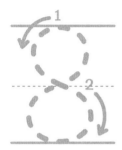

"Make an S, do not wait, go back up and close the gate."

Trace the 8's:

Count and circle the number of fruits there are.

	1 2 3 4 5 6
	1 2 3 4 5 6
	1 2 3 4 5 6

Creative Thinking:

Color the shapes below with the colors from the graph. Then count them for your graph and fill in. The first one is done for you.

"WOW! You two have grown!" exclaimed Mom as she recorded the twins' height and weight on the door frame of Grandma's screened porch.

Charlie had grown 2 inches and gained 4 pounds while Charlotte had grown 1¾ inches and gained 3 pounds. "That's a lot since we measured you just a few months ago." The twins grinned happily at how much they had grown.

"Mama, do you think we are big enough to ride Peanut?" Charlie hopped from one foot to the other. "Dad said that we have to big enough to reach the horn of the saddle when it's on Peanut's back, before we could ride!"

"I don't know, Charlie. Why don't you two get your coats, hats, and boots on and go ask Daddy," Mom said smiling down at her excited children.

"Whoopeeeeee!" Charlie howled in glee. "Come on, Charlotte!" The twins ran to put on their coats, hats, and boots, and with excited chatter, ran out to find Dad. After explaining to him that Mom had just measured them, the children asked if they were big enough to ride the pony all by themselves.

"I don't know, kiddos!" Dad answered. "The only way to find out is to try! You two go carry the saddle out from the tack room — make sure to bring the saddle blanket as well. And bring the bridle as well. Make sure you get the small curb bit, not the snaffle," Dad instructed the children. They ran off to get everything.

"Dad, this saddle is too heavy for me to carry. Will you help us?" called Charlie as they tried to lift it from the saddle rack.

"Sure," Dad replied coming to lift the small, leather western saddle from the rack, handing the saddle blanket to Charlie to carry and the bridle to Charlotte.

The twins remembered the Bible story about David putting on Saul's armor and how heavy it must have been, especially if a pony saddle was this heavy. Charlie grunted, "Dad, could you help me again?" He was having difficulty tightening and buckling the girth on Peanut's saddle around the plump pony's middle.

As Dad helped Charlie with the girth, Charlotte stood by watching and holding the bridle. Peanut's teeth looked a lot bigger and sharper than she remembered! It sure was a lot of work getting a saddle on a pony, Charlotte thought to herself. *Someday I'll be big and strong enough to do it by. . . .* Suddenly, Charlotte jumped and gave a startled yelp. A long spider's web was flying in her face and sticking in her hair. "Charlie look!" exclaimed Charlotte as she showed Charlie the web.

"Isn't it amazing how strong and stretchy a spider's web is?" Dad asked as Charlie and Charlotte nodded. "This is one way God shows us how something small can be strong. Like Peanut here. He's small for a horse, but he's strong enough to carry you two on his back! Who wants to go first?"

Calendar:

☐ Complete the calendar.

☐ Review on back of calendar.

Application:

Number of the Week:

9 — N-I-N-E spells nine.

This is the number 9. Count the 9 spiders.

When we write a 9, we start at the top line:

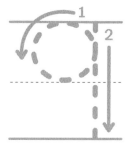

"Over, around, down to the line, that's the way we make a 9."

Trace the 9's:

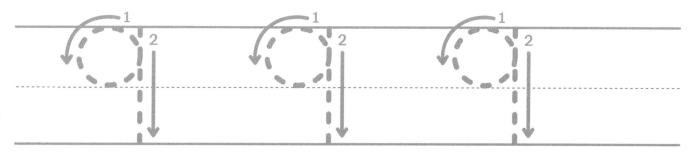

Critical Thinking:

Bees are very busy workers. Bees flap their wings 200 time per second which is what gives them the buzz sound. Bees make 12 collection trips a day, and visit 500–1000 flowers on each trip. They work almost non-stop from sunrise to sunset. They only stop for a 30-second nap if they need a break. They make honey, which is known as a miracle food. It contains almost every nutrient for life — and it won't spoil for years, even thousands of years! Archaeologists have found pots of honey in ancient Egyptian tombs and it's still good to eat! Isn't it amazing that God gave us bees and honey to help us?

Trace and color the 9 petals of the flower.

Application:

Number of the Week:

9 — N-I-N-E spells nine.

This is the number 9. When we write a 9, we start at the top line:

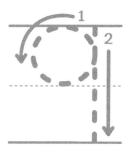

"Over, around, down to the line, that's the way we make a 9."

Trace the 9's:

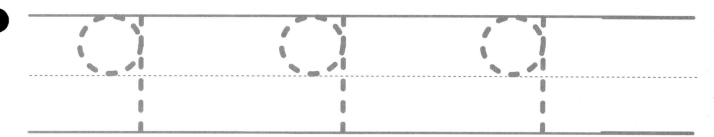

Trace and count. Color in the squares for the amount of each number.

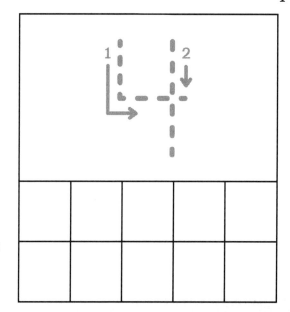

Critical Thinking:

When we look at a scale like this, called a balance, it kind of looks like a teeter totter! If the item weighs more, it pushes the scale down.

Tell your teacher which one weighs the most.

Application:

Number of the Week:

9 — N-I-N-E spells nine.

Let's practice writing the numbers we have learned so far.

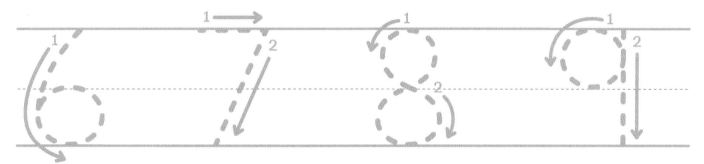

Let's trace these.

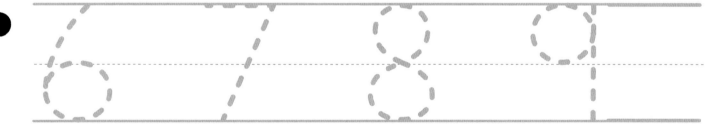

Color the number 9.

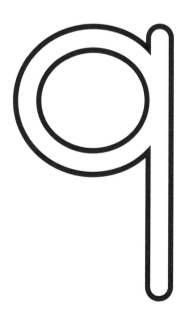

Name_____

Name_____

Critical Thinking:

Help the 9 find her correct box of bananas by tracing the right path.

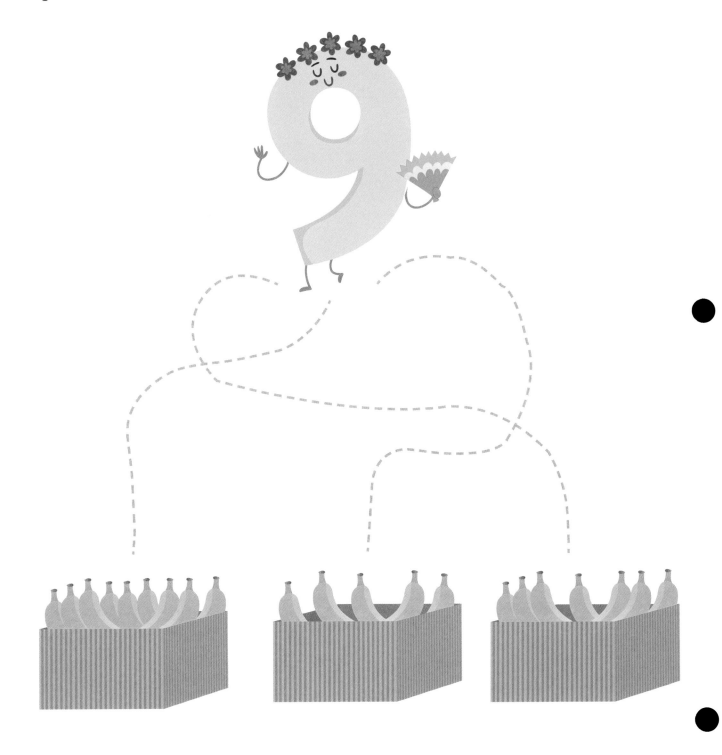

Name________________________________

Application:

Number of the Week:

9 — N-I-N-E spells nine.

Let’s practice our numbers. Try writing the number next to the one you traced.

6 7

8 9

Circle the 9’s.

9 3 7 6
4 5 2 9 1
0
8 9 8

Critical Thinking:

Spider webs barely weigh anything.

Use thread to make a circle around a globe or ball.

If you had a spider web that went around the earth, it would only weigh a little over 1 pound (16 oz.). That is barely over the weight of a loaf of bread. Spider webs are also very strong. The webbing is tougher than steel, but more flexible than nylon! In the South Pacific Islands, they even use it for fishing.

Remember, spider webs do not weigh a lot. Which web would weigh the most? Circle it.

Application:

Number of the Week:

9 — N-I-N-E spells nine.

This is the number 9. When we write a 9, we start at the top line:

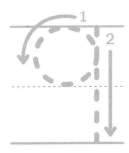

"Over, around, down to the line, that's the way we make a 9."

Trace the 9's:

Count and circle the number of faces there are.

	1 2 3 4 5 6
	1 2 3 4 5 6
	1 2 3 4 5 6

Critical Thinking:

Help the spider finish its web.

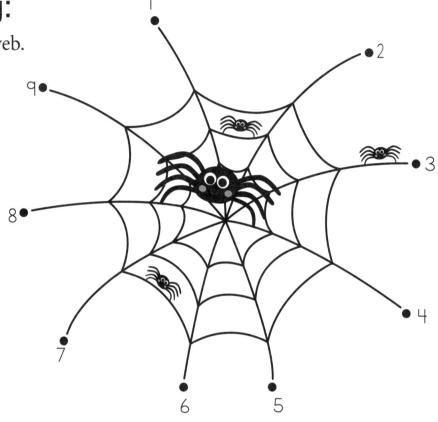

Which one is heaviest? Which one is lightest?

Number of the Week: 10, and Completing the Sequence

"Would you two like to help me do some grocery shopping?" Mom came into the room as the twins were coloring in their coloring books. "Wow, you two! These are so well done! Great work. If you two would like to come with me, go put your coats and boots on quickly. I'm going to go start the car. Charlotte, please brush your hair, Honey — it's rather tangled looking."

"Yes, Mama!" Both of the twins hopped down from their chairs next to the desk where they had been drawing.

Charlie stopped and thought for a minute. "Did Mama tell us to put on our shoes, or our boots?" He had not been listening carefully and couldn't remember what his mom had said after, "Would you two like to help me do some grocery shopping?"

Charlotte paused, too. "Ummm. I don't know! I remember her saying for me to brush my hair . . ." Charlotte answered hesitantly. The two of them were still standing there when their mom came back in from the garage.

"Why are you guys still standing there? Go do as I told you please! The car is running," she reprimanded the children.

"But we don't remember what you said," Charlotte responded with a quiver to her voice.

"Okay, I'll help you," Mom's tone softened as she laid her hand on her daughter's head. "First, I told you to put on your coat and boots, and then I told you to brush your hair. I suppose that could be kind of confusing!

You should brush your hair first, and then put your coat and boots on. Actually, if either of you need to use the restroom, you should probably do that first." At the look on her children's face, Mom stopped. "Okay, let's start over. Which do you think you should do first?"

Charlie and Charlotte looked at each other and then held up one of their fingers.

"First, we should use the bathroom." Charlie said holding up one finger.

"Then we should brush our hair," Charlotte added and held up two fingers.

"Right! Then we should put our boots on," Charlie smiled and held up three fingers.

"And then put our coats on!" finished Charlotte, and both twins held up four fingers.

Mom smiled. "Yes! Now you have it! That makes sense. You two go do those things in that order, and I'll grab a snack for you to have on the way to the store!" They all laughed and held up all four fingers and added their thumb for five.

Calendar:
☐ Complete the calendar.
☐ Review on back of calendar.

Application:

Number of the Week:

10 — T-E-N spells ten.

This is the number 10. Count the 10 butterflies.

When we write a 10, we start at the top line:

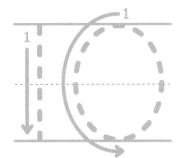

"10 is one then zero, that's the way to make a 10."

Trace the 10's:

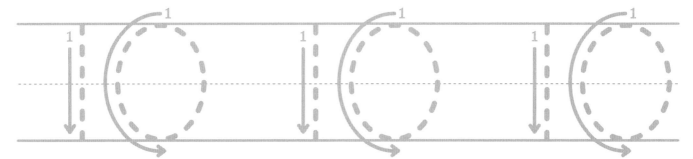

Critical Thinking:

Number Maze.

Color the numbers from 1–10 to help the bunny find the carrot.

1	2	6	5
8	3	7	4

3	9	5	4	10	1
1	7	6	2	8	5
4	8	9	10		
5	4	2	3		

Application:

Number of the Week:

10 — T-E-N spells ten.

This is the number 10. When we write a 10, we start at the top line:

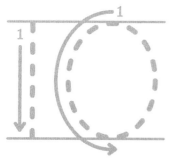

"10 is one then zero, that's the way to make a 10."

Trace the 10's:

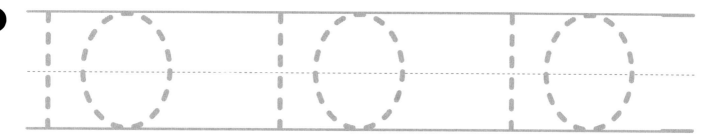

Which group has 10? Circle it.

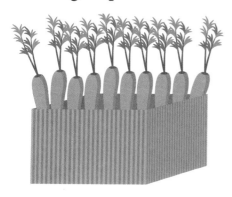
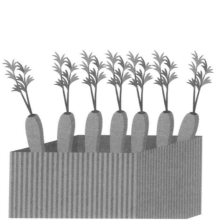

Critical Thinking:

Remember, a sequence helps us see the order of events. It tells us what happened first, second, third, and so on. It helps us recall facts too.

Sequence the pictures:

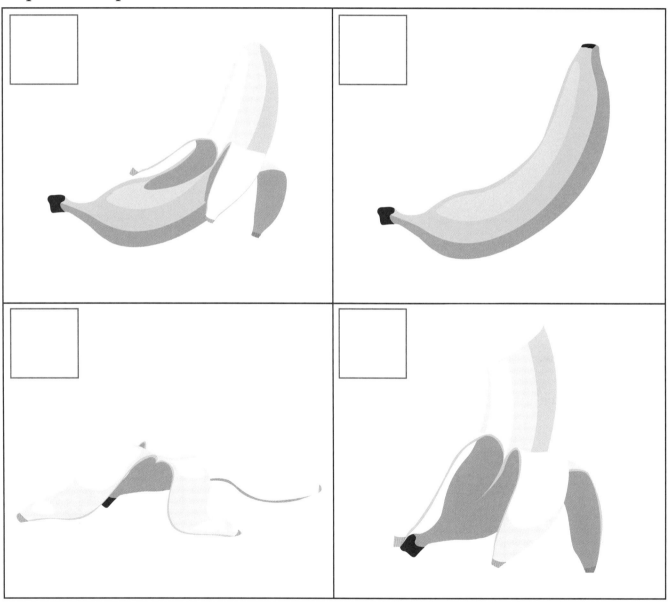

Application:

Number of the Week:

10 — T-E-N spells ten.

Let's practice writing the numbers we have learned so far.

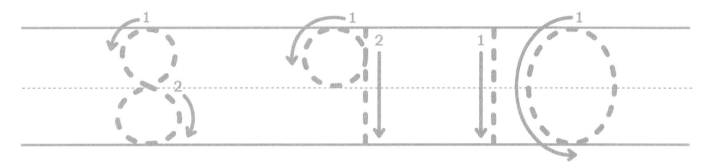

Let's trace these.

Color the number 10.

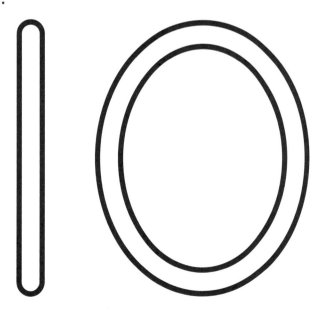

Critical Thinking:

What is a sequence?

Sequence the pictures:

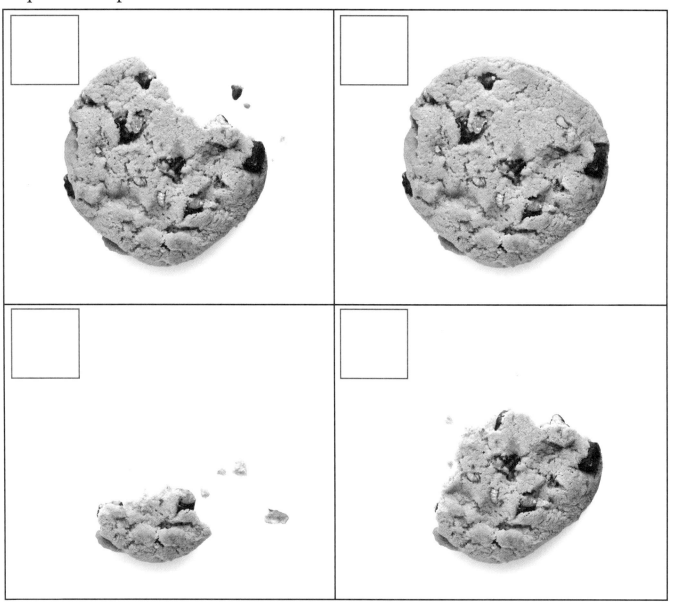

Name______________________________

Application:

Number of the Week:

10 — T-E-N spells ten.

Let's practice our numbers. Try writing the number next to the one you traced.

7 8

9 10

Circle the 10's.

10 3 7 6

4 5 10 9 1

0

10 9 10

Critical Thinking:

Find 10 differences.

Application:

Number of the Week:

10 — T-E-N spells ten.

This is the number 10. When we write a 10, we start at the top line:

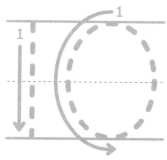

"10 is one then zero, that's the way to make a 10."

See if you can trace the ten then write two on your own.

Trace and count. Color in the squares for the amount of each number.

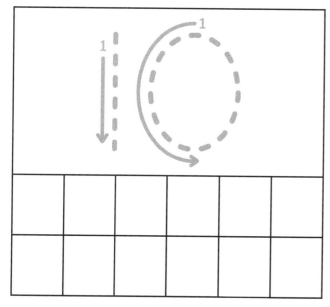

Critical Thinking:

Help Charlie by ordering the events of his day.

"Mom, what kind of birds are they?" asked Charlie. He and Charlotte had scattered some wild bird seed on the patio and now they were watching a flock of cute, little birds pecking away at it.

"Those are black-cap chickadees." Mom stood behind the children taking some pictures of the birds. "They are the kind of birds that stay all winter because they have beaks that allow them to eat hard-shelled seeds and nuts. Many other birds have to fly south for the winter, but chickadees stick around if they can find the food."

"Mama, can we draw a picture of the chickadees?" Charlotte asked. "Oh no! They all flew away! Now we can't draw them." The children were extremely disappointed.

"Don't worry, guys," Mom quickly reassured them. "I have a whole bunch of pictures you can choose from. Look," she quickly scrolled through a series of photos on her phone. "Here, I'll send these to the computer, so you can see them more easily. You two go get your drawing paper and art supplies and bring them to my desk. I'll open the pictures on my computer so you can choose which one you want to use."

The children scrambled to obey their mother. With art supplies and paper spread out before them, they clicked through the pictures, studying each one carefully.

"Look, Charlie, this one shows the whole flock of them," Charlotte pointed to the picture, "but this one shows the details of one of them. Do you want to draw the whole flock? Or do you want to draw a close-up of one of them?"

Charlie thought hard before answering. "I'll draw the whole flock. One, two, three, four, five, six, seven, eight, nine . . . and ten. There are ten birds in this picture. That's kind of a lot, but I can do it! Do you want to draw the close-up one, Charlotte?" Charlie asked.

"Sure! Let's leave both of the pictures open, so we can see them both," Charlotte agreed and began to carefully sketch the bird in the picture. "These little guys are so cute!" she exclaimed. "They look like they're wearing little black hats!"

The children worked quietly for a few moments. They were glad that the chickadees stayed around even for the colder months. They planned on making sure they had enough food to survive the winter.

Calendar:

- ☐ Complete the calendar.
- ☐ Review on back of calendar.

Application:

Circle 10 birds.

Count to 10 as you hop like a bird.

Critical Thinking:

Color the same number of circles as the number in each row.

1

2

3

4

5

6

7

8

9

10

Application:

Reviewing Numbers:

Roll the die and build a tower with that amount of blocks.

Trace the numbers as you say them aloud.

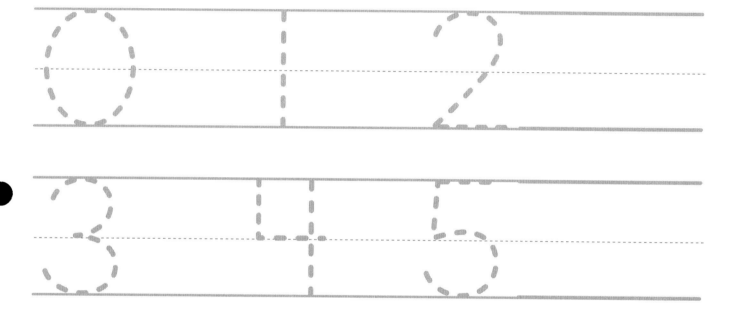

Count the birds below.

Critical Thinking:

How many birds did Charlie and Charlotte count in the picture? Draw some of them here.

Application:

Count the birds.

Count the birds and write the number below.

Count to 10 as you walk like a penguin.

Did you know that penguins are birds, but they do not fly?

Critical Thinking:

Put a triangle on the beak of 10 birds.

Roll and build. Roll the die and build a tower with that amount of blocks.

Application:

Count how many of each bird there are and write it in the box.

How many birds can you count outside?

Count to 10 as you flap your wings like a bird.

Did you know that hummingbirds move their wings over 1,000 times per minute? How fast can you beat your arms in one minute? They also have long tongues to lick up nectar in flowers.

Critical Thinking:

What number am I?

I am the number that tells how many fingers you have.

I am the number of beaks a bird has.

I am the number of wings a bird has.

I am the number of birds Charlie and Charlotte saw on their patio.

Application:

Reviewing Numbers:

Trace the numbers as you say them aloud.

Count and match:

          6

          4

          2

          |

Critical Thinking:

Point to the group of birds with 6 in it and say six.

Point to the group of birds with 5 in it and say five.

Point to the group of birds that has the fewest birds in it.

Point to the group of birds that has the most birds in it.

Review Counting, and Right and Left

"Charlie, your shoes are on the wrong feet again. Doesn't that feel funny?" Charlotte glanced down at her brother's feet. She could tell that he had them on wrong because the toes were pointing out away from each other. "You have the left shoe on your right foot, and the right shoe on your left foot." She added with a giggle.

"Hey. Don't make fun of me, Charlotte!" Charlie scowled at his sister. He was a little mad that she never got her shoes mixed up. "I can't help that I have a hard time getting my shoes on the right feet sometimes." He scowled again at his shoes. Mom had been working with him to help him remember his left and right. She had shown him that when he held up his left hand with his thumb sticking out, his pointer finger and his thumb created a capital L, which stood for left. Mom had also shown him that if he laid his hand in this position on top of his left shoe, the toe of the shoe — where his left big toe would be — was under that pointer finger, and the curved-in part, where the arch of his left foot should be, would be under the capital L of his hand. All of this made sense, but Charlie often did not want to take the time to do this little "is-this-my-left-shoe?" exercise.

"Charlie, didn't Daddy write an L on the bottom of your left shoe and an R on the bottom of your right one last night?" Charlotte reminded him.

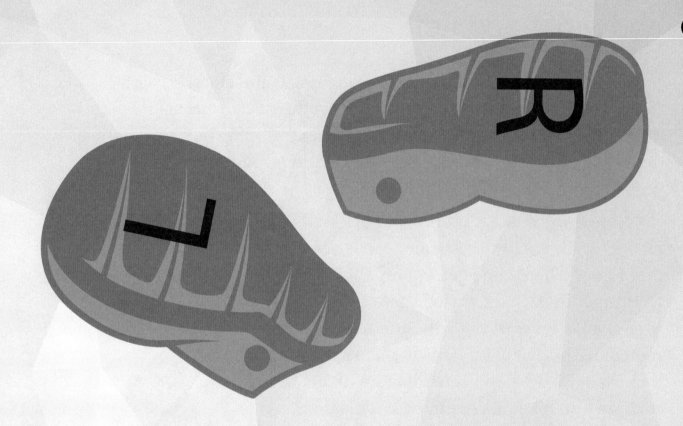

"Oh yeah!" Charlie sat down and pulled his shoes off. He looked at the bottom of each one. Sure enough, the one with the L for left had been on his right foot. Quickly switching his shoes to the correct feet, Charlie tied the laces and hopped back to his feet. Much better! It sure was nice to know his left from his right.

Calendar:

☐ Complete the calendar.

☐ Review on back of calendar.

Application:

Review Counting:

Count the shapes below and write how many there are.

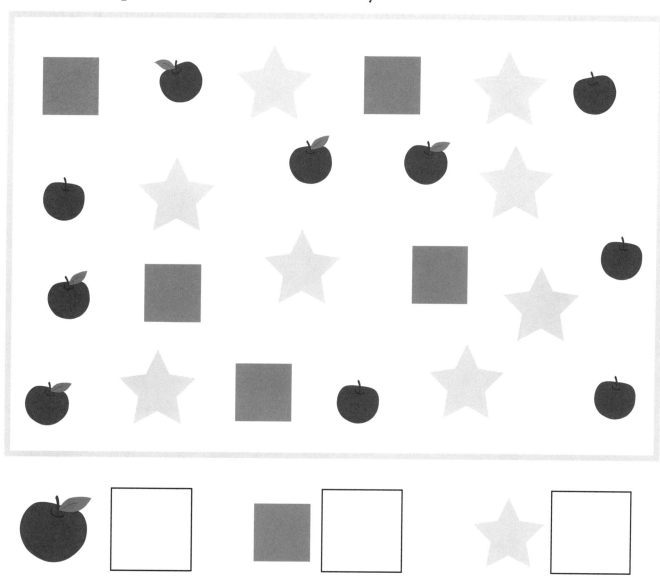

Count to 10 as you do wall push-ups.

Teacher
Have student put feet out from wall a little bit, hands flat on wall (body will be diagonal to floor), push wall like you are trying to move the wall as your body pushes out from wall.

Critical Thinking:

Left and Right game:

Have your student stand with arms at their side. Tell them which arm is left and which is right. Call out left or right as they raise that arm straight out to the side. Mix it up and have fun!

Teacher *Best if done outdoors. You might want to stand in front of them or to the side to model this as you do it.*

Application:

Review Counting: Count to 10 as you march around the room.

Reviewing Numbers: Trace the numbers as you say them aloud.

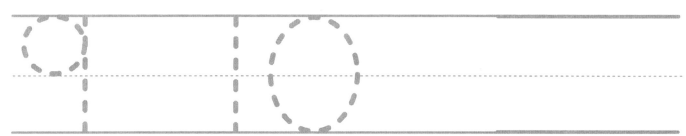

Count and match:

2

3

6

5

Critical Thinking:

Left and Right mix-up game:

How many left & right?

Math Level K – Lesson 27

Application:

Use the code to color the apples.

RED — 1 dot ●   GREEN — 2 dots ●●   YELLOW — 3 dots ●●●

Critical Thinking:

Left and Right mix-up game:

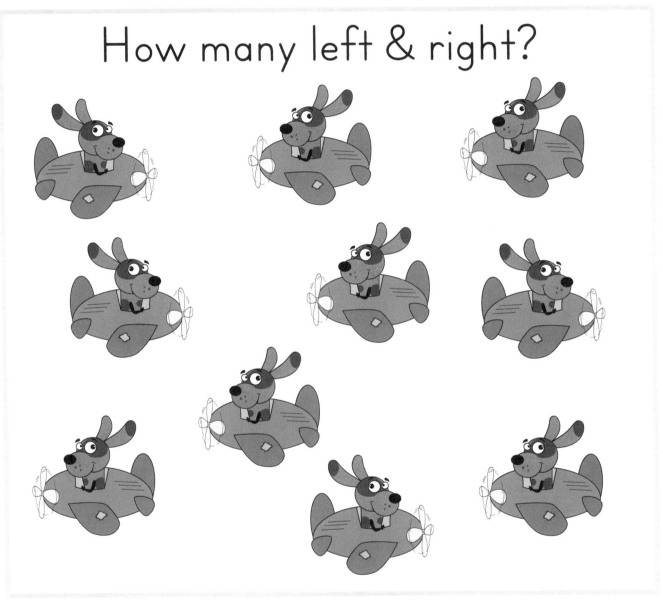

How many left & right?

Application:

Match the apples to the number.

1

2

3

4

5

Critical Thinking:

Match the direction.

Application:

Fill in the missing number.

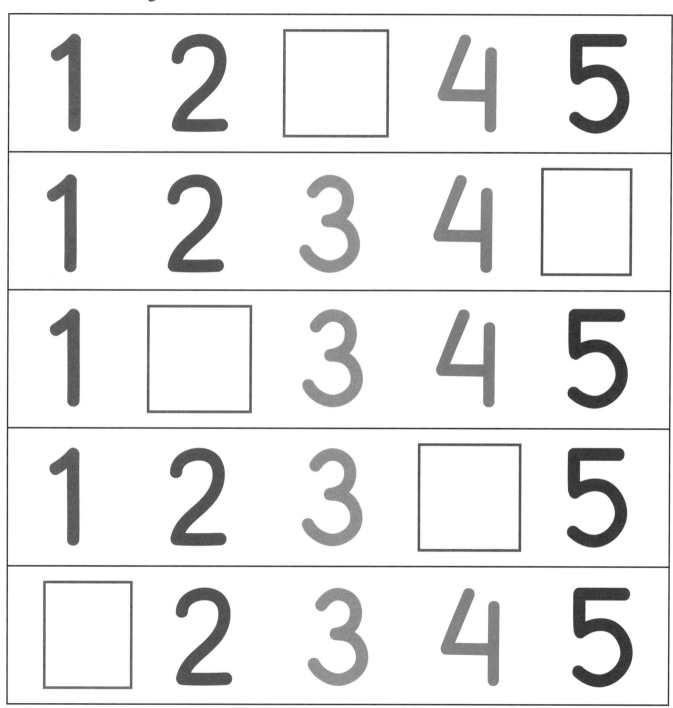

Critical Thinking:

Left and Right mix-up game:

How many left & right?

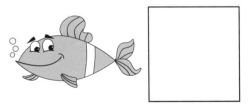

Review Numbers, and Patterns and Sequences

"Father says: hop on your left foot!" Dad called to the twins. The family was having a family game night, and it was Dad's turn to choose the game. Much to the delight of the twins, he had chosen "Father, May I?" their favorite game. Dad sat on the couch on one end of the family room, while the twins and Mom lined up on the opposite end. Dad called out commands for them to obey, but they had to listen carefully! If he said "Father says" before his command, they had to answer with "Father, may I?" before obeying the command, and he would answer "Yes, you may!" If he didn't say "Father says" before the command, they didn't obey the command at all. Sometimes, they forgot to listen for the "Father says" or they forgot to say "Father, may I?" Whoever forgot had to go all the way back to the starting point! Whoever reached Dad first, won the game. It was so much fun!

"Father says: hop forward on your right foot three times and cluck like a chicken at the same time!" Dad called out. They all looked at each other. "Father, may we?" they all shouted back together. "Yes, you may!" Dad answered.

Hop, hop, hop, cluck, cluck, cluck! Mom, Charlie, and Charlotte all hopped forward on their left foot three times, each time adding a cluck, cluck, cluck!

"March forward four steps — one for each time I clap!" Dad's eyes twinkled.

March, march, march, march.... "Mama! Daddy didn't say 'Father says!'" The twins collapsed onto the floor giggling. Mom hadn't listened closely and now she had to go all the way back to the beginning!

"Oh no!" Mom giggled until she almost cried. "Back to the beginning with me!"

"Okay, you two, Father says: march forward four times — once for each time I clap!"

"Father, may we?" they both shouted back.

"Yes, you may!" March, march, march, march. Clap, clap, clap, clap!

"We won!" The twins jumped up and down and high-fived their parents.

Calendar:

☐ Complete the calendar.

☐ Review on back of calendar.

Application:

Trace 0–10:

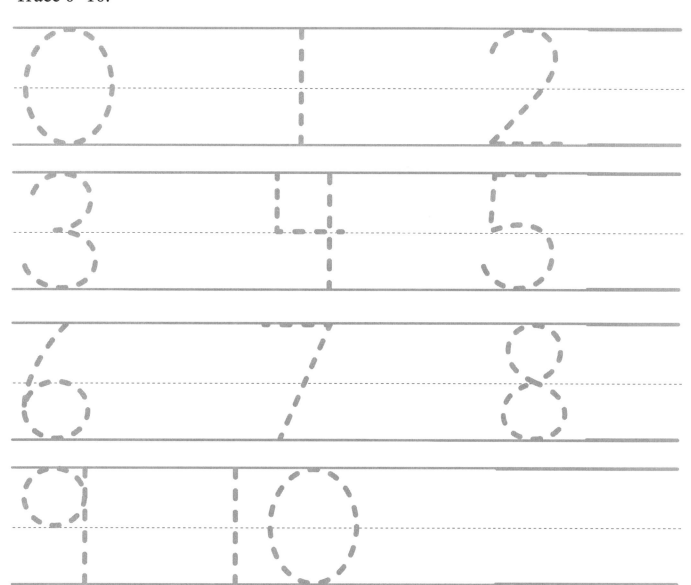

Use small items you find in nature or toys to place that amount of objects near each number. Hop and count on your number line from 0–10.

Critical Thinking:

Sound Patterns Game:

I will make sounds in a pattern or sequence, and you have to repeat the pattern.

1. Using the pot/pan, tap 3 times. Have them do it exactly like you.

2. Tap 2 times on the pan, once on the table/ground.

3. Tap 1 time on the pan, once on the table/ground, once on the pan.

4. Tap 2 times on the pan, 2 times on the ground, 1 time on the pan, and 1 time on the ground.

Teacher

All of this helps with working memory, patterns in a sequence, and auditory skills. Materials needed: pot/pan, wooden spoon.

Make a number line using painter's tape/post-its, or sidewalk chalk.

Teacher

Have the student draw the numbers.

| 0 | 1 | 2 | 3 | 4 | 5 |

Application:

Fill in the missing numbers.

0 1  3 4  6  8 9

Trace and count. Color in the squares for the amount of each number.

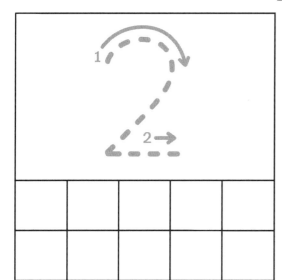

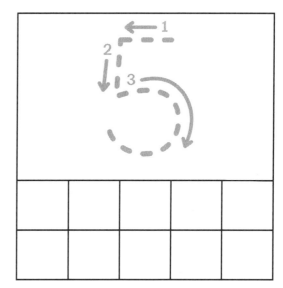

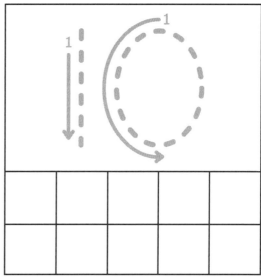

Critical Thinking:

Sound Patterns Game:

Today we will play our sound pattern game by clapping and patting our legs. Find a seat or sit on the floor so we can pat our legs.

1. Pat legs 3 times, clap 3 times.

2. Pat legs 1 time, clap 3 times, pat legs 1 time, clap 3 times.

3. Clap 2 times, pat 3 times, clap 2 times, pat 3 times.

Application:

Review 1–10:

Complete the number maze by coloring in from 1–10 to get the moose to the caboose.

8	7	4	5
1	2	3	6
14	13	12	9	8	7
15	5	11	10

Critical Thinking:

Sound Patterns Game:

Today we will use our feet and hands.

1. Stomp feet 2 times, clap 2 times, hop 2 times.

2. Clap 1 time, stomp 1 time, hop 1 time, clap 2 times, stomp 1 time.

3. Clap 2 times, stomp 3 times, clap 2 times, stomp 3 times.

Application:

In the boxes on the right, place these numbers in the correct order.

6
8
7
5
1
0
2
4
3
9
10

Critical Thinking:

Sound Patterns Game:

Reverse roles and you make up the pattern and your teacher will copy your sound pattern.

Instead of only doing sound patterns, add in movement patterns. Example: If you clap, take a step forward, and then wave. Have them mimic you.

Application:

Trace 0–10:

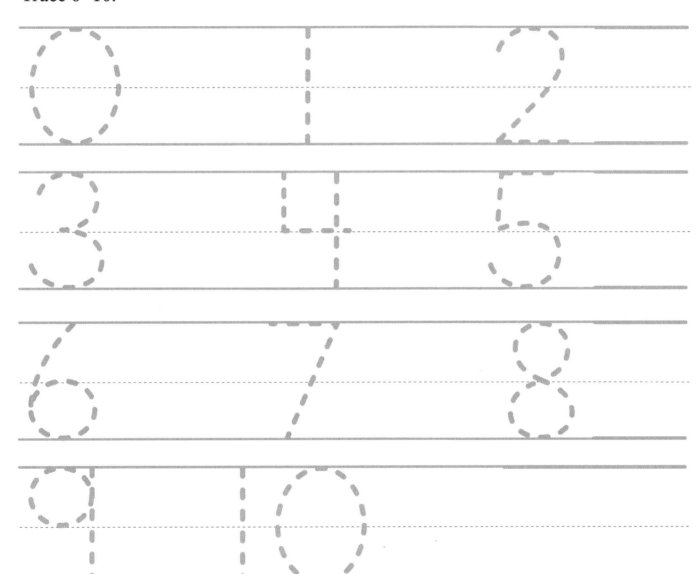

Critical Thinking:

Help 10 find their correct group of balloons by tracing the correct path.

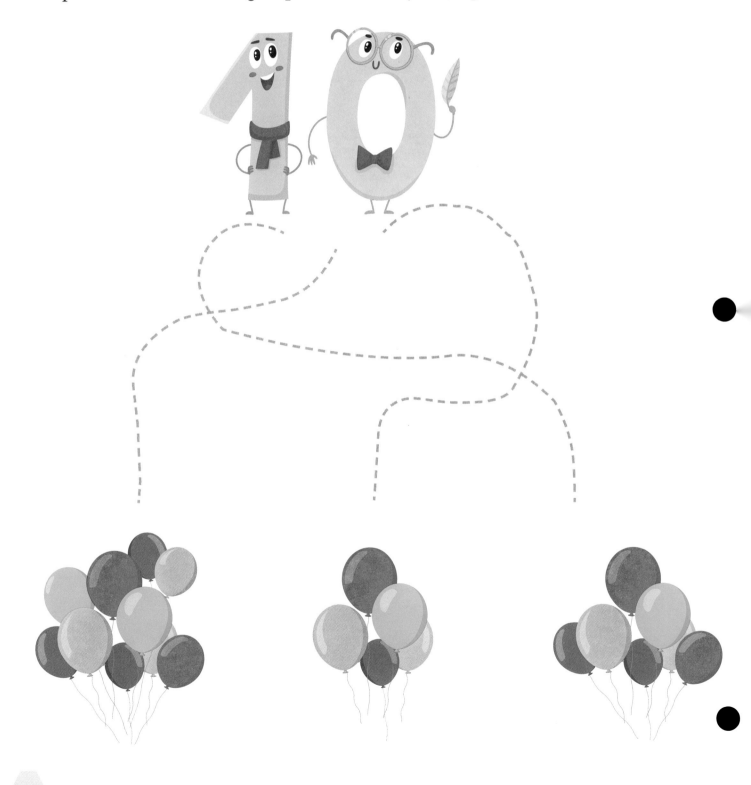

Sorting and Matching

"Come on, Charlie, you can do it!"

Charlie nodded in concentration. His feet rocked back and forth, as he swung his body in rhythm. He and Charlotte were practicing their hula-hooping skills in the basement game room. Grandma Violet had bought them each a new hoop, and they were determined to master it in the next week.

"Okay, my turn!" Charlotte grabbed her hoop and moved to the middle of the open space. "Watch me, Charlie!" Her brother nodded and moved to a beanbag chair to rest. Charlotte moved back and forth. This was a lot harder than it looked when Mom showed them how to do it earlier. Mom had hula-hooped for five minutes straight without dropping her hoop! She told the children that she had once won a hula-hooping contest when she was a young teenager.

"This is really hard to do, isn't it, Charlie?" Charlotte sighed. She had made her hula-hoop twirl exactly four times before it clattered to the floor.

Charlie nodded. "Let's go ask Mom if we can have a snack." Charlie hopped over the hoops on the floor and scampered up the steps. "Mama, can we have a snack?" he called as he ran.

"Actually, you may have lunch — and please don't run on the stairs, Charlie!" Mom nodded to the table, where she had already begun placing items for lunch. "After lunch, I am going to show you both how to do a new chore! So, eat up," she ruffled Charlie's hair as she placed his plate in front of him. "Hmmm. Did you two wash your hands? No? Well, you skedaddle and do that first!"

"What's our new chore, Mama?" Charlotte asked between bites of grilled cheese sandwich. "Is it something grown-up?"

"Very grown-up, Charlotte," Mama smiled. "In fact, it's so grown-up you have to promise that you will be extremely careful doing it, so you don't get hurt." Her eyes twinkled.

The twins looked at each other with big eyes. How exciting! After they finished their lunch, Mom had the twins join her at the dishwasher. Up until now, they had not been allowed to touch the dishwasher. Now, Mom explained to them how they were to never try to open the dishwasher when it was running. In fact, they were to wait until she had turned the special dishwasher magnet on it from the "dirty/washing" side to the "clean/finished" side. She carefully instructed them how to open the appliance and pull out the racks, one at a time. Mom explained how important it was that the twins be careful not to break anything, and also to put it away in the right place so it could easily be located.

"All of the drinking glasses go in this cupboard — right side up. All of the dinner plates go in a stack here in this cupboard, and the bowls are sorted by size — the cereal bowls here, the soup bowls here, and the serving bowls over here. All of the silverware goes in this organizer. See? The bigger forks here, the smaller ones here, the soup spoons here, and the tea spoons here. All of the serving spoons go here. Do you understand?"

The twins nodded. This really was an important job, and one that took some mad sorting skills! They really must be growing up for their mom to trust them with this new chore.

Calendar:

☐ Complete the calendar.
☐ Review on back of calendar.

Application:

Sorting is putting things together that are alike or the same.

> **Teacher**
>
> *Materials needed: Hula hoops, some blue toys, some red toys, and some blue and red toys (or books).*

We will sort toys/objects by color first. If they are red, they go on the red side of the circle. If they are blue, they go on the blue side of the circle. But what happens if they have both red and blue? The go in the middle where the circles overlap.

Begin sorting the objects now.

Critical Thinking:

Using the same objects, organize by two attributes. First, sort them by color.
Then, sort them by size as well. So, you will have 4 piles when you are done.

Application:

Remember — sorting is putting things together that are alike or the same.

Match each apple to the correct basket based on the shape of the apple.

Critical Thinking:

Draw a line to match the shapes.

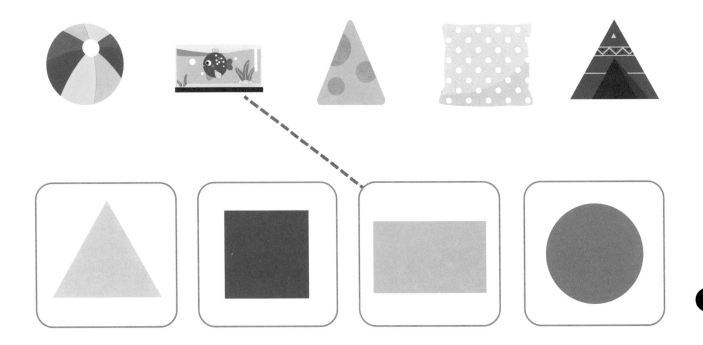

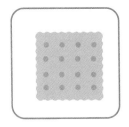    

Application:

Remember — sorting is putting things together that are alike or the same.

Draw a line to sort which items are hot or cold:

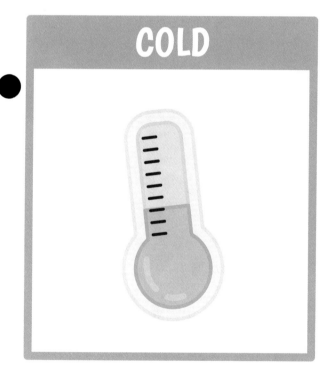

COLD

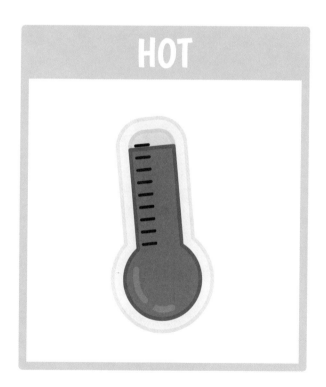

HOT

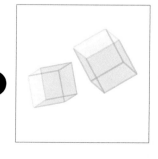   

Critical Thinking:

Draw a line to sort the animals by whether they live on land, in water, or both.

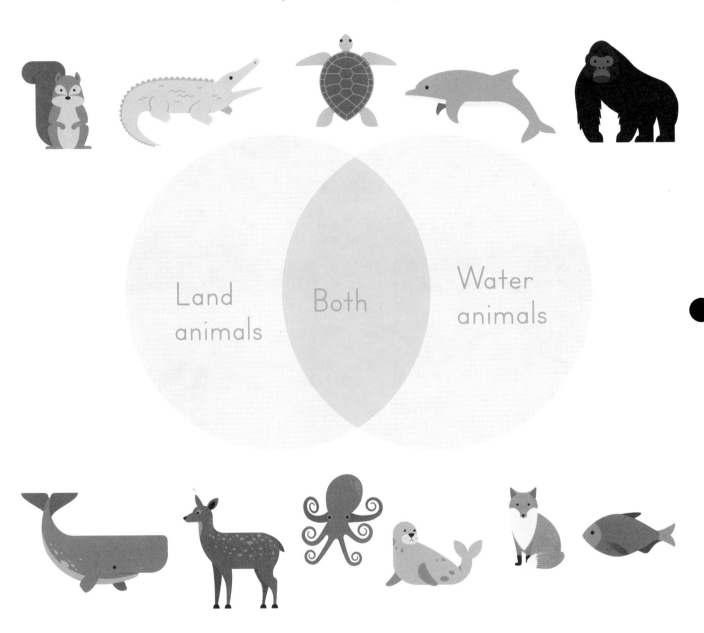

Application:

Draw a line to sort which items are circles or squares:

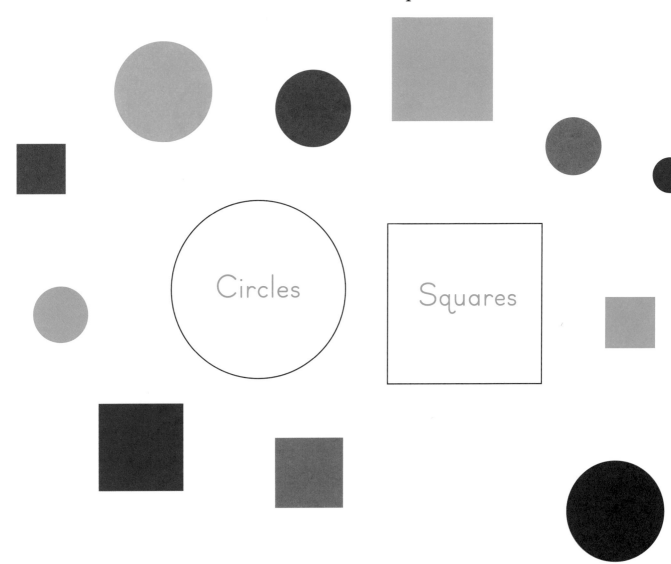

Critical Thinking:

Draw a line to sort the things by whether they are animals, things that fly, or animals that fly.

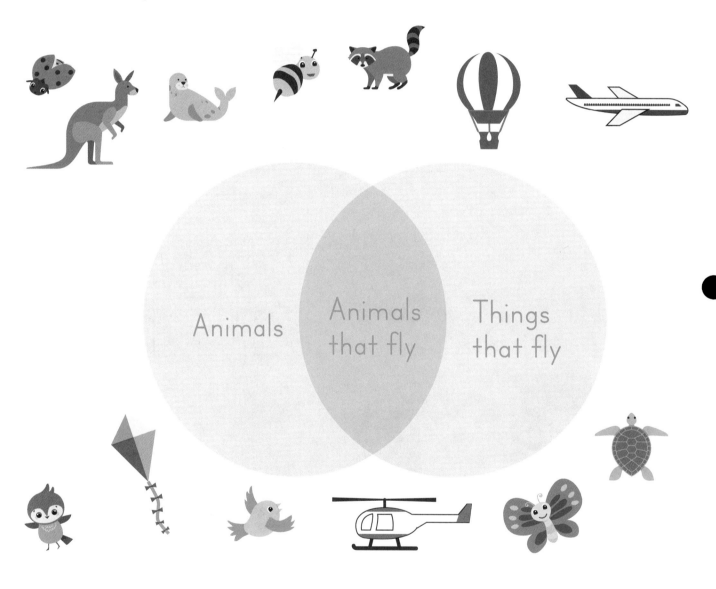

Application:

Remember — sorting is putting things together that are alike or the same. Draw a line to sort which objects are heavy or light.

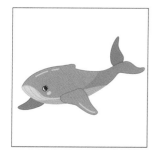   

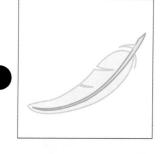   

Critical Thinking:

Draw a line from the objects to where they belong in the night, the day, or both.

Review Shapes and Matching

One Saturday morning, the twins were working hard in their room. Mom had given them the chore of sorting and organizing their toys. She had given them each a tub to fill up with toys they had outgrown. As they cleaned and organized, they chattered about what to do with the toys. They had decided to donate some of their "too-young" toys to the church.

"Mama, can we take these tubs with us to church tomorrow and give them to the lady in the nursery?" Charlotte snapped the lid down on the tub and then sat on top of it. It was kind of sad to see so many of her old toys go, but she knew that they couldn't keep everything they had gotten since they were very little. Mom had a strict rule about not having too much stuff to take care of. In fact, she always said that if the twins received new toys as a gift for Christmas or for their birthday, they had to get rid of something to make room for the new things — they couldn't just add the new to what they already had.

Charlie didn't like to get rid of anything, but he knew he couldn't argue with Mom about this. He had tried that once and had ended up losing all of his toys for two whole days. Besides, it was good to give to those in need.

"Charlotte, let's play with some of our new toys before Mom calls us for lunch," Charlie smiled bravely. Maybe playing with something new and shiny would get his mind off of the old toys under the lids in the bins. "First, let's drag these out in the hall and out of the way." Together, the children scooted and pushed the tubs out into the hall.

"Charlie, let's play with these!" Charlotte requested. "I love creating and building stuff!" The twins pulled open the lid on a large container of brightly colored wooden blocks in all kinds of shapes and sizes.

"Yeah! Let's build a robot!" Charlie had already mostly forgotten the toys in the hall.

Together, the twins used every single block to make a robot. Their new friend was created out of squares, triangles, circles, and rectangles. What fun it was to put him together!

Calendar:

☐ Complete the calendar.

☐ Review on back of calendar.

Application:

Shapes Review:

How many shapes do you see?

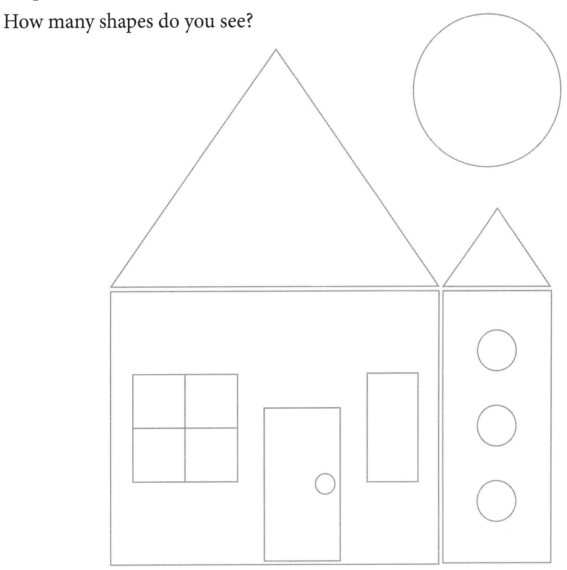

_____ = △   _____ = ▯

_____ = ○   _____ = ▢

Critical Thinking:

Make a shape friend below using circles, triangles, rectangles, ovals, and squares.

Application:

Shapes Review:

Match the shapes to the object:

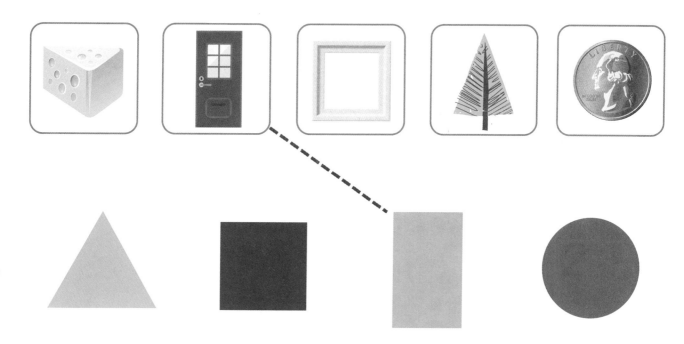

Critical Thinking:

Trace and color the shapes as directed:

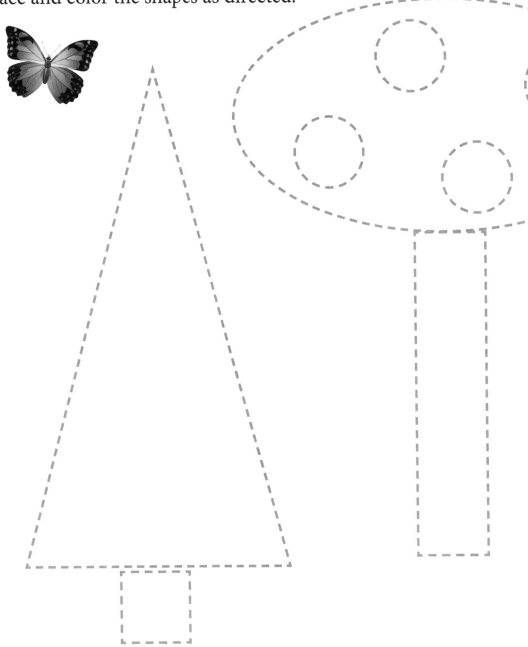

Rectangles – Brown

Squares – Grey

Triangles – Green

Ovals – Green

Circles – Red

Application:

Shapes Review:

Draw the correct shape in the space provided:

Trace the shape	Join the dots	Try by yourself
☐	• • • •	
△	• • •	
▭	• • • •	
○	(dots in circle)	

Critical Thinking:

Shape hunt.

Find one item for each shape and show your teacher.

Square, circle, triangle, oval, rectangle

Application:

Shapes Review:

Color and count the shapes using the key.

Color	
🎃	orange
▲	yellow
■	green
▬	blue
●	red

Count	
🎃	
▲	
■	
▬	
●	

Critical Thinking:

Using craft sticks and glue, make a square, triangle, and rectangle. Then, cut gift tissue paper to the size and glue it on. Hang with a string/yarn.

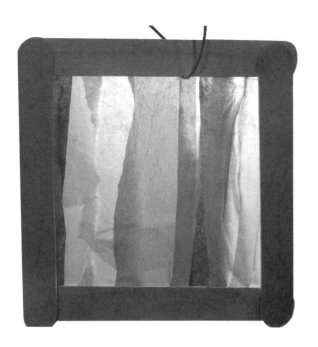

Application:

Shapes Review:

Count the corners and sides and write the number.

Picture	Name	Number of Corners	Number of Sides
△	Triangle		
○	Circle		
□	Square		
▭	Rectangle		

Critical Thinking:

Who Am I?

We will play a game about our shapes! I will describe a shape and you have to guess what shape it is. Say it as soon as you guess which one it is.

- I have 3 sides. You might see me on the tops of houses.

- I have 4 sides. I am the shape of a door.

- I have 10 sides. You might find me in the night sky.

- I have 4 sides. All of my sides are the same size. I am the shape of a computer key.

- I have 4 sides, but not all have to be the same size. If you fly a kite on a windy day, I am there.

Answers: triangle, rectangle, star, square, diamond

Concepts of Time: Morning, Afternoon, Evening, and Night

"Children, we are hosting the church small group meeting this week, so that means you and your friends can have a game night in the basement," Mom informed the children one morning at breakfast. "There will be two older girls, Clara Adams and Jennifer McDonald, to help watch everyone down there."

"What games can we play, Mama?" Charlotte asked. "We have some new ones. We could play those with our friends!"

"That's very kind of you, Charlotte," Mom answered. "Now, you two go work on your chores, while I clean up the kitchen. I have a list of cleaning projects that I would like to get through this morning."

"Yes, Mama," the twins replied and ran to get their chores finished. Maybe they would have time to clean up and organize the game room before their friends came over later.

The game night finally came, and all went well … at least for a few minutes!

"But I want to win the game!" Charlie stomped his foot and crossed his arms over his chest. "It's not fair, Clara! It's MY game!" Tears began to drip down Charlie's face and off of his chin. He brushed them away angrily.

"But Charlie, everyone played the game by the rules," Clara Adams tried to reason with the angry boy. "We can't just say that you won, when you didn't!"

"It's not fair!" Charlie shrieked, grabbing the board game off of the table and throwing it on the floor, causing an eruption of protests from the other children gathered around him.

"I'm going to go get Mama," Charlotte told the two older girls who were doing their best to calm the situation. Both of them nodded their heads.

"Charles, you stop that noise immediately," Mom's voice brought Charlie's yelling to an instant halt. "What on earth are you doing? Get up right now and stand on your feet." Mama looked at him and then turned to the two older girls. "What is going on here?" she asked them.

"We're so sorry, Mrs. Stevens, but Charlie started throwing a tantrum when he lost the game we were playing," Jennifer said looking like she was on the brink of tears herself.

"It's okay, Jennifer . . . Clara. His behavior is not your fault," Mom reassured the girls. "Charlie, no one wins all of the time. It is unkind to expect others to always allow you to win at every game. You must learn to be happy for those who do win — that is called 'being a good sport.' And it's an important part of the 'love your neighbor' commandment that Jesus gave us. Your attitude is showing selfishness, Charlie. You need to ask for forgiveness from your friends for being unkind and ruining the game."

Charlie sniffed and nodded. He knew that his behavior was not nice. He went around the circle and asked each of them to please forgive him . . . everyone did. He felt embarrassed and ashamed of his actions. From now on, he would try to be a good sport.

Calendar:

☐ Complete the calendar.

☐ Review on back of calendar.

Application:

Each day, we have words we use to describe the time of day without giving an exact clock time. When we wake up, we call that *morning*. We continue to say morning until around lunchtime, then after lunch we say *afternoon*. Later in the day, around dinner (supper) time, we call that *evening*. This is about when the sun is setting. And last, when the sun is down, we call this *nighttime*.

Look at the pictures below. Can you show me a picture that might be morning?

Which picture shows afternoon? What about evening? And which one shows night?

Critical Thinking:

What time of day is it? Riddles:

What time or times of the day do you brush your teeth?

What time of day do you eat lunch?

What time of day do you get on your pajamas?

What time of day do you see the sun rising?

Application:

Remember the terms *morning, afternoon, evening,* and *nighttime*? Put these pictures in the correct order from morning to nighttime.

Critical Thinking:

What did you eat this morning? Draw a picture of it here:

Math Level K – Lesson 31

Application:

Circle morning ☀ or evening ☽ to tell what is your routine. It might be both!

Critical Thinking:

Draw lines to match each picture with its shadow.

Application:

Circle whether you do this during day ☀ or night ☾.

DREAM	school work	Talk on the PHONE
☀ ☾	☀ ☾	☀ ☾
Look at the STARS	Go to the LIBRARY	SNORE
☀ ☾	☀ ☾	☀ ☾

Critical Thinking:

Draw a picture of what you do in the morning, during the day, and at night.

Morning	Day	Night

Application:

Review:

Let's practice our numbers. Try writing the number next to the one you traced.

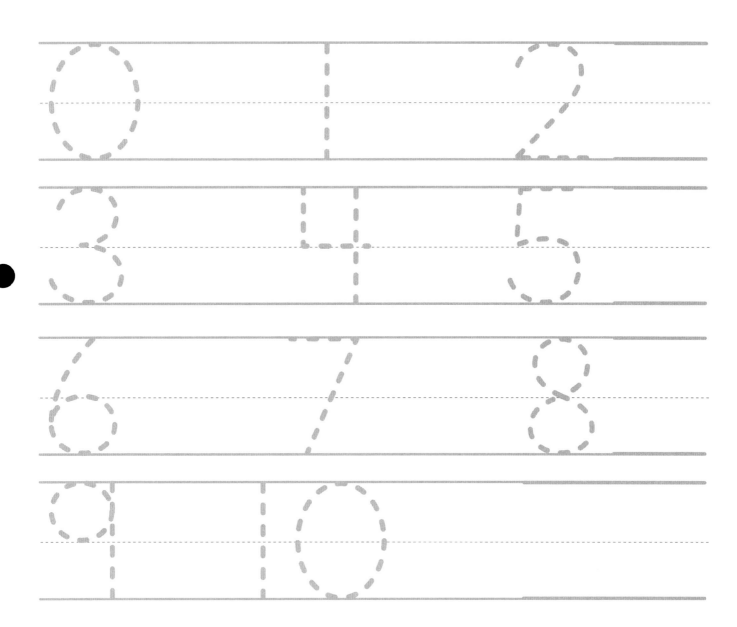

Name________________________________

Exercise 5 Day 155

Critical Thinking:

Let's think about the morning, the afternoon, the evening, and the night. In the four spaces below, draw pictures for each time of day.

Morning	Afternoon
Evening	Night

"Today is Mama and Daddy's anniversary, Charlie! Aren't the flowers that Daddy bought for Mama beautiful? Mama said that there are 18 long-stemmed red roses in the bouquet." Charlotte chattered on about how the roses smelled so nice. Charlie and she were making cards for their parents' anniversary. A babysitter was coming soon to watch the children while their parents went out to dinner. Mama and Daddy promised to come home before the twins' bedtime though, so they could all enjoy a special dessert together.

In the dining room, the children marveled at how long the stems on the beautiful roses were. "Mom, how long are these flowers?" Charlie asked. He had never seen such long stems before! The flowers had been delivered to the house in a long, white box tied with a huge pink bow. They had come by a special delivery truck. Dad had surprised Mama with them, ordering them to be delivered at precisely 1:12 in the afternoon — the exact time that they had exchanged their wedding vows eight years ago. As the twins watched Mom open the box of flowers, they were shocked! They had never seen such beautiful flowers in their entire lives. The blooms were as big as their hands, the leaves were bright green and shiny, and the stems seemed almost as long as the twins were tall!

"Mama, how long are those stems?" Charlotte exclaimed. "Are they as long as I am?"

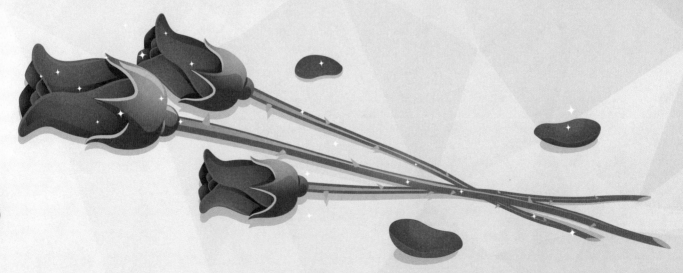

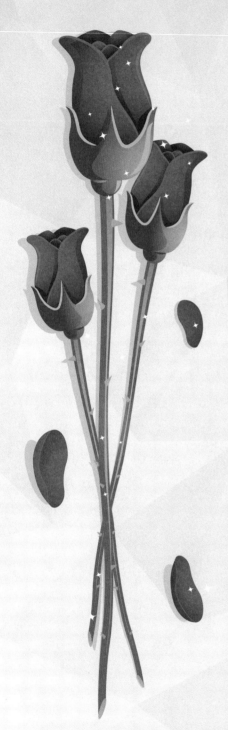

"No, Charlotte," Mama chuckled. "I don't think they are as long as you are. Come here, I'll show you. Now, be careful, these still have thorns on them. Hold still. . . ." Mom carefully held the rose up to Charlotte like a measuring stick. "See? You are 1½ roses tall!" Everyone giggled. It was fun to measure each other with things that weren't really measuring devices.

The evening before, the children had helped Dad make Mom's favorite dessert — apple crisp. Dad said that it was something he had made for her every single year for their anniversary because she loved it so much. The children were surprised that there was no recipe for the dessert! Dad simply gave them instructions to "measure" a "dash" of cinnamon, a "pinch" of salt, and a handful of flour, and another handful of oatmeal, while he peeled and sliced a mound of apples. He knew exactly what it was supposed to look and smell like, and he added this and that until it was deemed "perfect!"

Calendar:

☐ Complete the calendar.

☐ Review on back of calendar.

Application:

Review:

Trace the shapes:

Tell your teacher what each shape is called.

Critical Thinking:

Do you remember when we talked about over and under?

What does it mean to go over something? (go above it) Show me how you can go over something. Show me how you can go in something. Show me how you can go around something.

over   under

on   in

around

Application:

Review:

Count out 10 blocks/counters.

Can you count to 10 while you hop?

Match the opposites:

cold

dry

up

down

strong

wet

weak

hot

Critical Thinking:

Take a block and do the following:

- Put the block on the book.
- Put the block below the table.
- Put the block beside the book.
- Put the block under the book.
- Put the block in front of you.
- Put the block behind you.

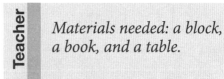

Teacher *Materials needed: a block, a book, and a table.*

Name_____

Application:

Review:

Count and graph the birds. Color in the graph when you know how many there are.

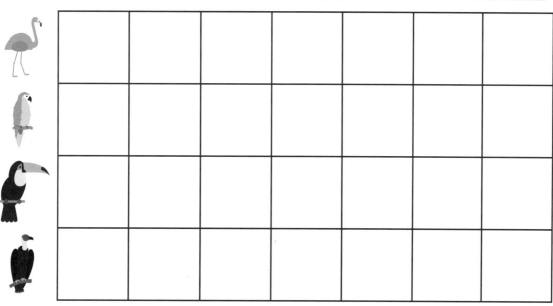

Critical Thinking:

Left and Right mix-up game:

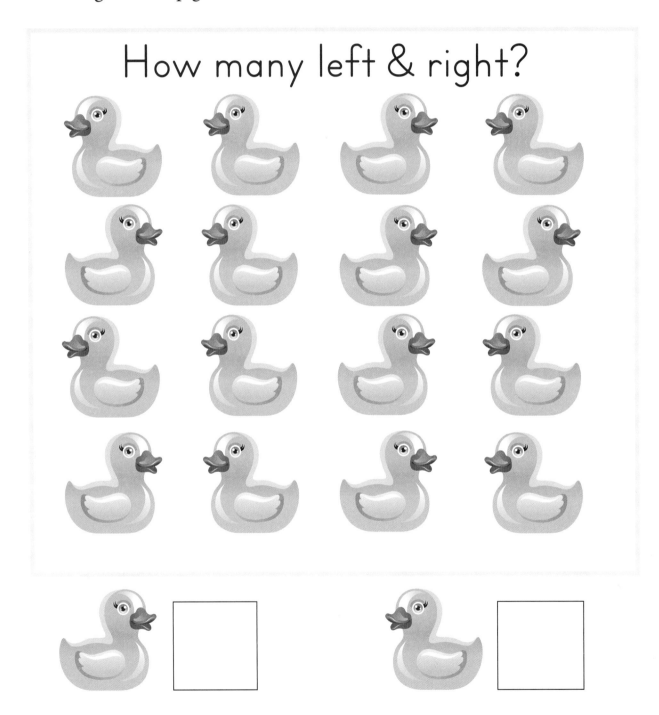

How many left & right?

Application:

Review:

Circle the one that is biggest:

Critical Thinking:

Let's measure these things with flowers. Tell how many flowers tall each object is.

Application:

Review:

Circle the one that is tallest:

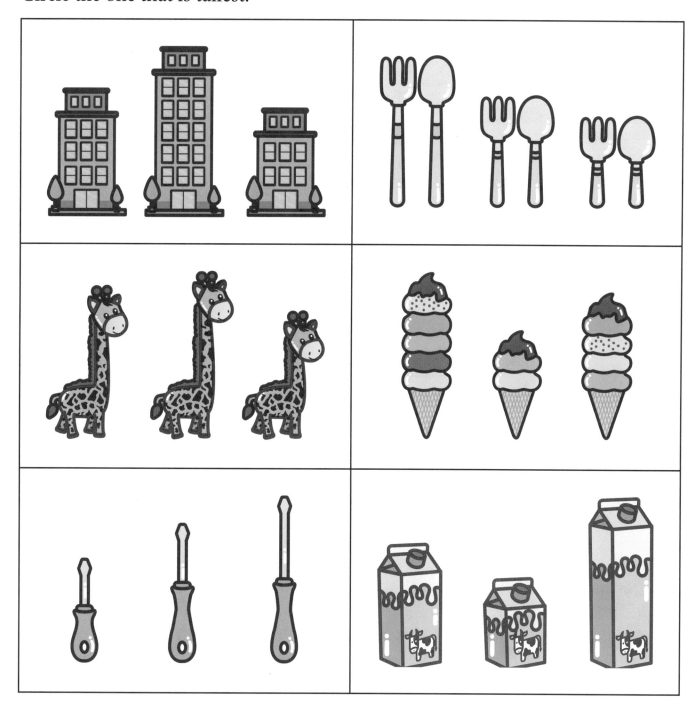

Critical Thinking:

Circle the tank with the **least** amount of fish.

Circle the **smallest** number.

3 5 2 4

Color the shape with **3** sides.

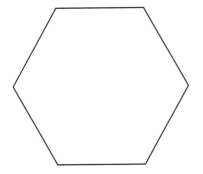  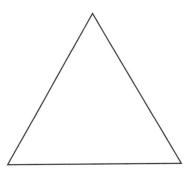

Color the dice red with the **smallest** number.

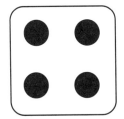   

Review Weights, Small and Large, and Comparisons

After breakfast, the children and their parents went to help at their church food pantry.

"Children, Mom and I think that you two are old enough to help us this time," Dad explained to them. "It is so important to have a giving heart and to be aware of those in need around us."

"Sean and Maddie, I can't tell you how wonderful this is of you to help out this morning," Mrs. Davidson said to Dad and Mom, as she smiled down at the twins. "I need to show you the different types of containers we have to pack food into to send home with the families who will come today. Now, we do our very best to set up the food pantry to make it similar to a store. We want the families who visit here to feel like they are shopping at a regular grocery store. We do not charge any money for the food, but if they want to donate what they can, they are welcome to do so. We know that it is very hard for some of these families to accept help, and we want to make sure they are honored in every way possible."

As the children helped their parents restock the shelves of the food pantry, they watched the families who came to receive food. They saw many of them with cloth shopping bags. The twins were familiar with these, because Mom and Dad kept a bin of them in the trunk of the car for impromptu shopping trips. Mom had showed them what kinds of containers are recyclable and what are non-recyclable. She had taught them not to waste their food. Both Dad and Mom had always taught the children that everyone must do their part to take care of the beautiful earth that God has given us as our home. By doing this, it brings the Creator God glory.

"Mom, can we play store tonight?" Charlie asked as the tired family drove back to their home that evening. It had been a very busy day, and they had stopped to pick up Chinese take-out for dinner. The aroma was making Charlie's stomach growl.

"Sure, Charlie," Mom smiled at him in the rearview mirror.

Calendar:

☐ Complete the calendar.

☐ Review on back of calendar.

Application:

Circle the scale that has the least weight on it.

1.

2.

1.

2.

Critical Thinking:

Circle the scale that has the most weight on it.

1.

2.

1.

2.

Application:

Good Stewards:

Time to weigh you! Let's compare how much you weigh versus how much items in a store weigh.

How much did you weigh?

How much did the sweet potato weigh?

Which one weighed more?

Weigh another person — which one of you weighs more?

Weigh a ball. Does the ball weigh more than the head of lettuce? Why do you think it weighs more/less?

Teacher

You can weigh the person with and without the ball to see what it weighs.

Sweet potato
½ pound

Critical Thinking:

Compare the objects in each row and write a 1 for the lightest, a 3 for the heaviest, and a 2 for the one in between.

Application:

Big or Little?

We have talked about how things are big or little or how things weigh more than others.

Circle the object that would weigh more than the other:

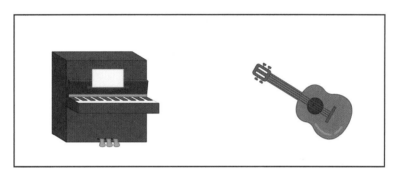

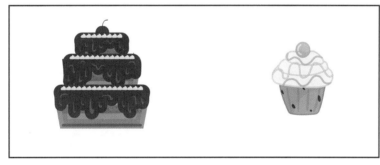

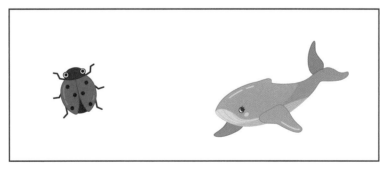

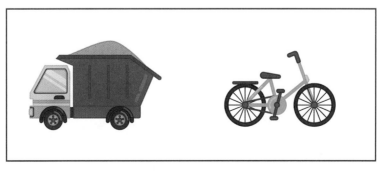

Critical Thinking:

Which weighs more?

Circle the one in each group that weighs the most.

Math Level K – Lesson 33

Application:

Number the images 1–4 to put them in order from smallest to largest.

Critical Thinking:

Lining up 1 to 10.

Teacher

Using clear glass jars/glasses, line them in a row. Place a post-it note with a number 1–10 in front of the middle jar. Have the student put that amount of buttons (or counters) in the jar. Have them use the post-it notes to place the number that comes before the number you chose on the jar on the left and add that amount of buttons/counters. Then, have them place the number that comes next on the jar on the right and put that amount of buttons/counters in that jar.

Example: 3 jars, jar in the middle has a 4 on it. The child places 4 buttons/counters in that jar, then finds the #3 on the post-it and places it on the jar to the left and adds 3 buttons. Then, they find the #5 and place it on the jar on the right and add in 5 buttons/counters.

Application:

Compare each object. Circle the one that is heavier.

Critical Thinking:

Draw some things you can do to be a good steward and take care of the wonderful world God made for us. Here are two ideas to help get you started.

Introducing Money, Patterns, and Shapes

The next day, after the family had returned home from church, Charlie and Charlotte began gathering items for a play store. Dad gave them a container that was full of change and a few paper bills of money. The twins did not know how to count money, but that was okay. Mama told them that when they were a little older, they would learn this important skill. Both of the twins were excited about this, but for now, they simply organized the coins in piles.

"Charlie, I never noticed that there were so many different kinds of coins, did you?" Charlotte stared closely at the pile in front of her. "And they all have faces on them! I wonder who they are."

"Yeah, these coins in this pile are so much smaller than those. I wonder what these are called. Daddy, can you come and tell us what each of these kinds of money are?" Charlie called to his dad, who was helping Mom in the kitchen.

"Sure, kiddo," Dad came in and ruffled Charlie's hair. "Those in front of you — the small ones — are dimes. And these," he pointed to the ones in front of Charlotte, "are quarters. These over here are nickels, and those are pennies."

"Daddy, why are there pictures of people on all of these?" Charlotte was kneeling in a chair, her elbows on the table in front of her and her face close to the coins so she could study them closely.

Dad grinned at her. "Those are portraits of important presidents of our country, the United States of America. You will learn about them when you get a little older." The twins sighed. It seemed like they had to wait until they were older to do everything. Dad saw their disappointment and asked, "Would you two like to learn about my favorite president on one of these coins?"

"Yes, Daddy! Please?" both of the twins jumped down from their chairs and came to hug their dad. Smiling, he took them by the hand and led them to his special chair, where he sat down and pulled each of them onto one of his knees.

Calendar:

☐ Complete the calendar.

☐ Review on back of calendar.

Application:

You will be a store owner this week and each day we will play store.

> **Teacher**
>
> *You will be making a pretend store. You can simply use items you have and place price tags on them. Help them set up a pretend store with items from around your home. Label each item with 1 or 2 cents.*
>
> *Materials needed: items from your pantry or toys from a bin, and pennies, nickels, and dimes*

Here is a penny.

(Lay out one penny for them to see as well.)

A penny equals 1 cent. When we count pennies, we count them just like we count blocks.

Count these pennies (set down all 10 pennies).

In your store, you have items labeled for 1 cent, or 1 penny. You have some labeled for 2 cents or 2 pennies.

Let's play store! I will browse and buy from your store.

Critical Thinking:

Patterns are all around us. God created animals with patterns, like zebras, or other things with patterns, like a spider web.

Look at this pattern.

Here is a circle (point to the 1st circle). Then, we have a square (point to the 1st square). Next, it goes back to a circle.

Notice how the pattern changes back and forth:
Circle-Square-Circle-Square-Circle-Square.

Look at this pattern and circle which shape would come next at the end.

     _____

Application:

Here is a penny.

<u>(Lay out one penny for them to see as well.)</u>

A penny equals 1 cent.

Here is a nickel.

A nickel is worth 5 cents. It is the same as 5 pennies.

Let's play store! I will browse and buy from your store.

Critical Thinking:

We will continue looking at one-two patterns.

Here is another pattern. Remember, patterns continue. Circle the correct object to finish the pattern.

Application:

Here is a penny.

<u>(Lay out one penny for them to see as well.)</u>

Do you remember how much a penny is worth? (one cent)

Here is a nickle.

A nickle is worth 5 cents. It is the same as 5 pennies.

Here is one dime.

A dime is the same as 10 pennies!

Let's play store! I will browse and buy from your store.

Critical Thinking:

Trace the pattern that comes next.

Application:

Here is a penny.

<u>(Lay out one penny for them to see as well.)</u>

Do you remember how much a penny is worth? (one cent)

Here is a nickle

<u>(Lay out one nickle for them to see as well.)</u>

A nickle is worth 5 cents. Do you remember how many pennies it is worth or the same as?

Here is a dime.

<u>(Lay out a dime for them to see.)</u>

A dime is the same as 10 pennies.

Here is a quarter.

<u>(Lay out a quarter for them to see.)</u>

A quarter is the same as 25 pennies.

Let's play store! I will browse and buy from your store.

Critical Thinking:

Patterns can also change by color. Here is an example of a pattern with the same shapes, but that changes by color.

Red heart-blue heart-red heart-blue heart-red heart-blue heart.

Now it's your turn. Color the shape to complete the pattern.

Application:

Here is a penny.

(Lay out one penny for them to see as well.)

Do you remember how much a penny is worth? (one cent)

Here is a nickle.

(Lay out one nickle for them to see as well.)

A nickle is worth 5 cents. Do you remember how many pennies it is worth or the same as?

Here is a dime.

(Lay out a dime for them to see.)

A dime is the same as 10 pennies!

Let's play store! I will browse and buy from your store.

Critical Thinking:

Complete the patterns in the space below. Color them if you like!

_____

_____

_____

Possible vs Impossible, and Review of Symmetry

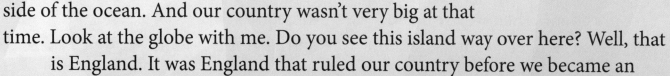

"I'm going to tell you the story of this man, right here." Dad held up one of the coins from the table. It was one of the bigger ones. "This is George Washington. He's important because he was our country's first president. But he was a much more than that! He was also the army general who helped our country become a country. You see, Charlie and Charlotte, our country used to belong to another nation . . . one that was way on the other side of the ocean. And our country wasn't very big at that time. Look at the globe with me. Do you see this island way over here? Well, that is England. It was England that ruled our country before we became an independent nation."

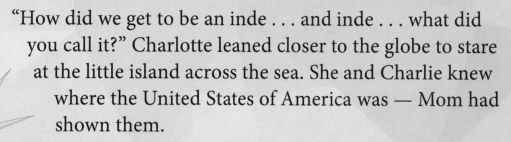

"How did we get to be an inde . . . and inde . . . what did you call it?" Charlotte leaned closer to the globe to stare at the little island across the sea. She and Charlie knew where the United States of America was — Mom had shown them.

"Well, we Americans had to fight for our independence, Charlotte. And that's where George Washington came in. He was the army general who led our soldiers in a war called the Revolution. At that time in history, America was just right here . . . much smaller than it is now, and there weren't many people who lived here! The English army was much bigger, stronger, and better trained. The rest of the world thought it was very unlikely that the Americans would win. In fact, many people thought it was impossible! But God had a plan for America. He had created men who would not give up and who would fight for our independence. With God, ALL things are possible. Nothing is too hard for Him! And He gave General George Washington the strength to do what needed to be done. This story teaches us an important lesson, kids. When we rely on God, things that seem unlikely or even impossible to humans, become very likely and possible. It was a long, hard war, but at the end, the United States of America became its own nation, and George Washington was elected as our first president. Then we grew a lot! All of these areas over here," Dad's finger swept around the area on the globe, "all of this became part of our country."

"Wow! It's no wonder George Washington's face is on this coin!" Charlie stared at the man's face engraved on the coin. He liked George Washington.

Calendar:

☐ Complete the calendar.

☐ Review on back of calendar.

Application:

Review Symmetry:

Symmetry is when we cut an object in half and both sides are the exact same. Remember when we looked at our shadows? What we have on the right side of our body is the same as our left side.

Draw lines to cut the objects into symmetrical pieces.

Critical Thinking:

We are going to be playing a game this week of Possible vs Impossible. *Possible* means it is able to be done by a person or thing; *impossible* means it is not able to be done by a person or thing.

I will say something and you tell me if it is Possible or Impossible.

- A bee will fly into a beehive.
- A dog will walk on water.
- A frog will hop into a pond.
- A pig will fly a kite.
- You will eat dinner.

We will keep playing this game in different ways this week.

Application:

Review Symmetry:

Draw a line to match the object with the match to make it symmetrical.

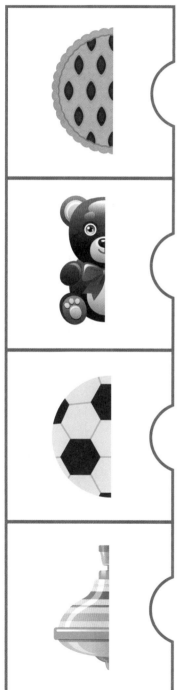

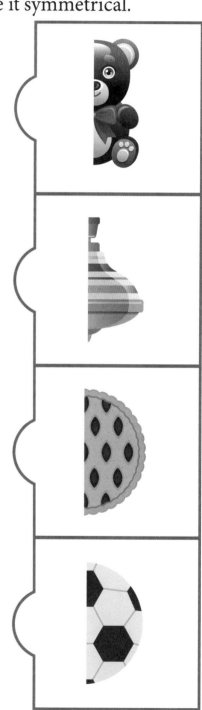

Critical Thinking:

We will play another round of Possible vs Impossible. Remember, *possible* means it is able to be done by a person or thing; *impossible* means it is not able to be done by a person or thing.

Possible or Impossible Chart:

Look at the pictures below. Your teacher will read the statement, and then you decide if it is Possible or Impossible.

Spider crawls on a web.	A dog cooks us dogs.	A moose rides a caboose.
Possible Impossible	Possible Impossible	Possible Impossible
A pig flies a plane.	A child plays guitar.	A bee leaves the hive.
Possible Impossible	Possible Impossible	Possible Impossible

We will keep playing this game in different ways this week.

Application:

Sometimes things may be possible, but not likely. Look at this example.

There are 2 red fish in this pond, and 8 blue fish.

Do you think it is more likely that I would catch a red fish or a blue fish? Right — it's more likely that I would catch a blue fish because there are more blue fish than red fish.

Your teacher will read the questions below, and then you will decide if it is "more likely" or "less likely."

How likely are you to grab a ★ ?

More Likely   Less Likely

How likely are you to grab a ▮ ?

More Likely   Less Likely

Critical Thinking

We will play another round of Possible vs Impossible.

I have 2 pieces of paper. One has an I for Impossible, and the other has a P for Possible. I will put them on opposite sides of the area. You will be in the middle of the papers. When I say something, you have to decide if it is Possible or Impossible and then run to P for possible or I for impossible.

Teacher *Materials needed: One piece of paper with an "I" and one piece of paper with a "P." Save pages for tomorrow as well.*

- A snail will hide in its shell.
- A dinosaur will be your next pet.
- You will go to sleep in your bed.
- You will drive a car to town.
- The birds will say "oink" and "moo."
- You will brush your teeth.
- A monkey will ride in a spaceship to Mars.

Application:

How likely?

Circle the fish you are more likely to catch.

Circle the fish you are less likely to catch.

Critical Thinking:

We will play another round of Possible vs Impossible.

I have 2 pieces of paper. One has an I for Impossible, and the other has a P for Possible. I will put them on opposite sides of the room. You will be in the middle of the papers. When I say something, you have to decide if it is Possible or Impossible and then run to P for possible or I for impossible.

- A frog will grow legs and walk.
- A dinosaur will fly.
- You will have a snack.
- You will play outside.
- A zebra will sing.
- You will wear socks.

Application:

Review Symmetry:

Draw a line to match the object with the match to make it symmetrical.

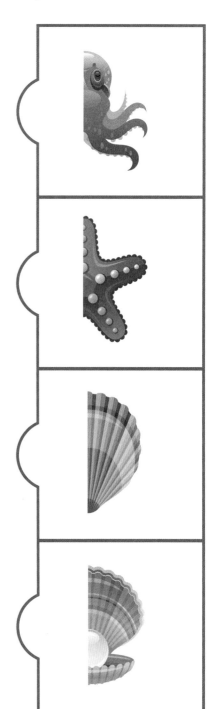

Critical Thinking

Is it likely or unlikely to get a red gumball? Circle your answer:

Likely   Unlikely

Ordering Numbers, Right and Left, and Review of Numbers 1–10

"Happy Easter, everyone!" Grandma Violet's cheerful voice greeted her family as they gathered around the large, dining room table. The twins and their parents had come to the farm to visit their grandparents for Easter. Outside, the ground was a rich brown, and all of the mama animals at the farm were having their new babies. It was spring!

"I can't believe we are already into April!" Mom exclaimed. "Time goes by so fast. The twins are growing up right before our eyes."

"Mama, what month is April? Is it number 3 in the year?" Charlie asked.

"Actually, Charlie, April is number 4. January is the 1st month, February is the 2nd month, March is the 3rd month, and April is the 4th," Mom answered him.

"You kiddos certainly are growing fast," Grandpa said. "You're getting old enough to do some big and adventurous things." Both of the twins turned to look at Grandpa Peter. He had that up-to-something twinkle in his eyes.

"What are you talking about, Grandpa?" Charlotte asked.

"Yeah, what's going on, Grandpa?" Charlie added.

"Well, kiddos, I think it's best if we let your parents explain, okay?" Grandpa replied. The twins looked at their parents. What was happening? There was excitement in the air.

"Charlie and Charlotte, Mom and I are going on a trip in a few weeks. We're going to be flying on a big plane down to Peru in South America. Remember when we showed you South America on the globe?" Dad waited for the twins to nod their answer before continuing, "Well, that's where we'll be. We'll be gone for quite some time — too long for you to come with us. Grandma and Grandpa are going to take care of you. You two are going to come stay here on the farm with them. What do you think of that?"

The twins sat silent for a moment. Their parents were going away for a long time? How was that a good thing? Charlotte blinked back her tears. She didn't want to stay at the farm while her parents were far away.

"Charlotte? Honey, are you okay?" Mama gathered the little girl onto her lap. "Honey, Daddy and I will call you every day. Remember how we do that with Grandma and Grandpa? We call them and talk with video chat?"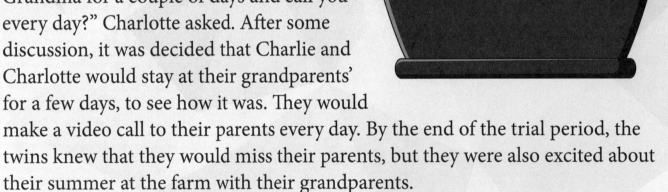

Charlotte nodded against her mom's chest. Maybe it wouldn't be too bad if she could see her parents every single day.

"Mama, can we practice? Can Charlie and I stay here with Grandpa and Grandma for a couple of days and call you every day?" Charlotte asked. After some discussion, it was decided that Charlie and Charlotte would stay at their grandparents' for a few days, to see how it was. They would make a video call to their parents every day. By the end of the trial period, the twins knew that they would miss their parents, but they were also excited about their summer at the farm with their grandparents.

Calendar:

☐ Complete the calendar.
☐ Review on back of calendar.

Application:

Review: Color the numbers from 1–10 to help the mouse find the cheese.

1	2	6	5
8	3	7	4

4	9	5	4	1	10
3	7	6	2	5	8
1	8	9	10		
5	4	2	3		

Critical Thinking:

Ordering things helps if we use words such as first, second, third, fourth, and so on.

When counting objects, the object we would say 1 for is also known as first. The object we would count as 2, would be second. The object we would say 3 for is also known as the third. The object we would count as 4 is also known as the fourth.

So, when counting objects,

- 1 is the first number
- 2 is the second number
- 3 is the third number
- 4 is the fourth number

Here is the FIRST or 1st object in this row.

Here is the SECOND or 2nd object in the row.

Here is the THIRD or 3rd in the row.

Here is the FOURTH or 4th object in the row.

Teacher

It is okay if this concept is not mastered. This is an introduction and something they will get more practice with. You might give hints, such as remember that first is also known as 1.

Which animal is first? Circle it.

Which animal is second? Circle it.

Which animal is third? Circle it.

   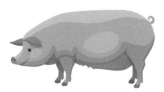

Which animal is fourth? Circle it.

  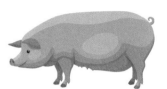

Application:

Review:

Let's practice our numbers. Try writing the number next to the one you traced.

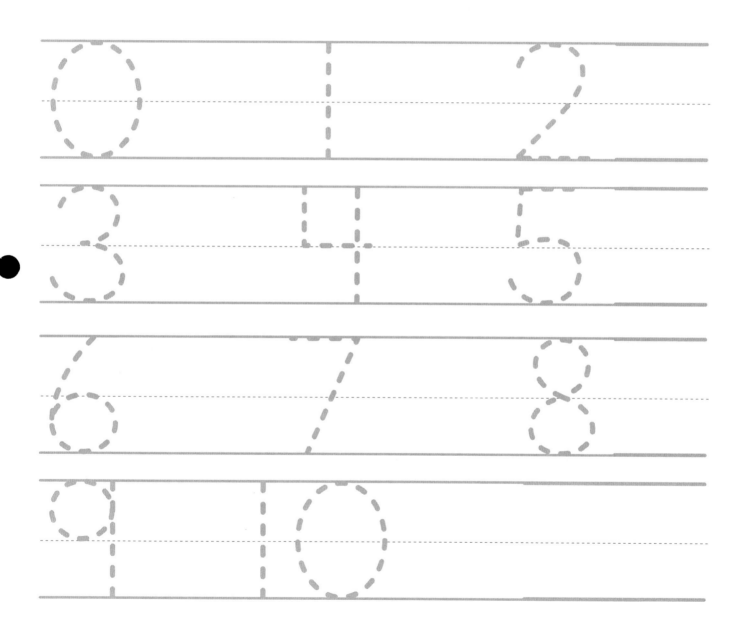

Critical Thinking:

Remember that when ordering objects we use the words first, second, third, and fourth.

- 1 is the first number
- 2 is the second number
- 3 is the third number
- 4 is the fourth number

Here is the FIRST or 1st object in this row.

Here is the SECOND or 2nd object in the row.

Here is the THIRD or 3rd in the row.

Here is the FOURTH or 4th object in the row.

Name_____

Color the shape that is first.

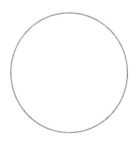 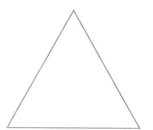  

Color the shape that is second. Circle it.

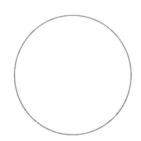 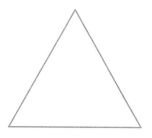  

Color the shape that is third. Circle it.

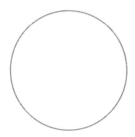 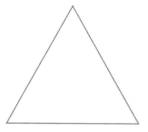  

Color the shape that is fourth. Circle it.

 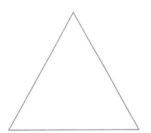  

Application:

Circle the correct missing ice cream scoop.

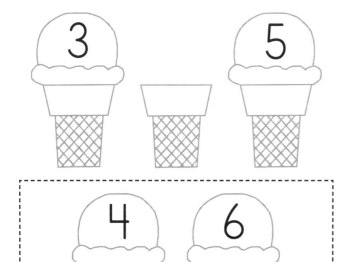

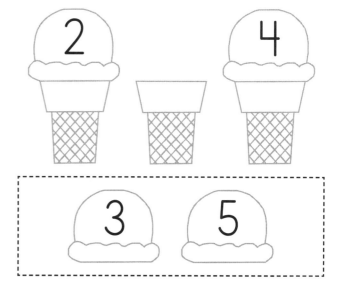

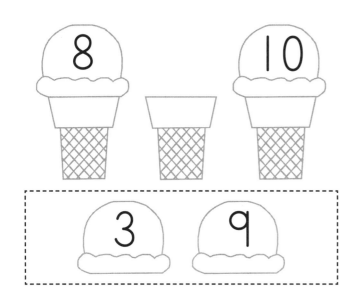

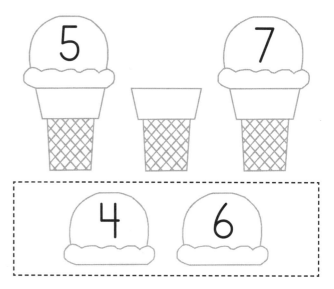

Critical Thinking:

Remember when ordering objects, we use the words first, second, third, and fourth.

- 1 is the first number
- 2 is the second number
- 3 is the third number
- 4 is the fourth number

Here is the FIRST or 1st object in this row.

Here is the SECOND or 2nd object in the row.

Here is the THIRD or 3rd in the row.

Here is the FOURTH or 4th object in the row.

Application:

Review:

Count how many cents:

= _____ ¢

Fill in the missing numbers.

Critical Thinking:

Above, on and below.

Draw 3 birds above the boat.

Draw 2 fish below the boat.

Draw 2 ducks on the water.

Application:

Match the apples to the number.

6

7

8

9

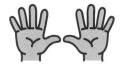

10

Critical Thinking:

Circle whether the animal is facing left or right.

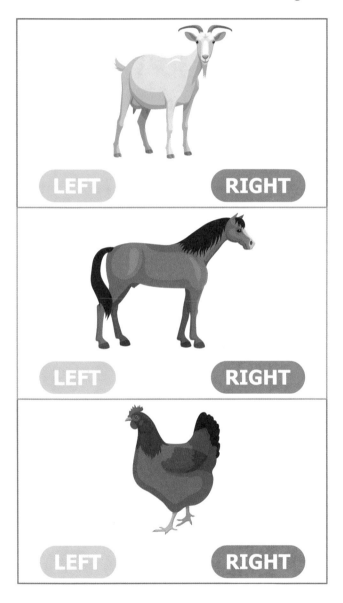

LEFT   RIGHT

LEFT   RIGHT

LEFT   RIGHT

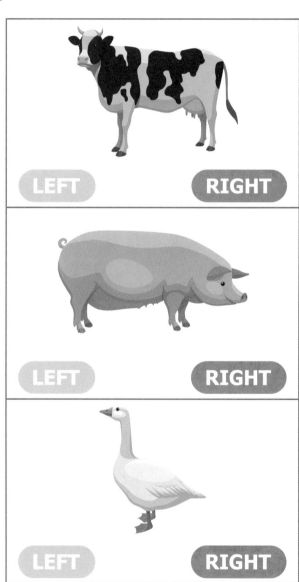

LEFT   RIGHT

LEFT   RIGHT

LEFT   RIGHT

Congratulations!
You have finished the course!

Number Practice Sheet

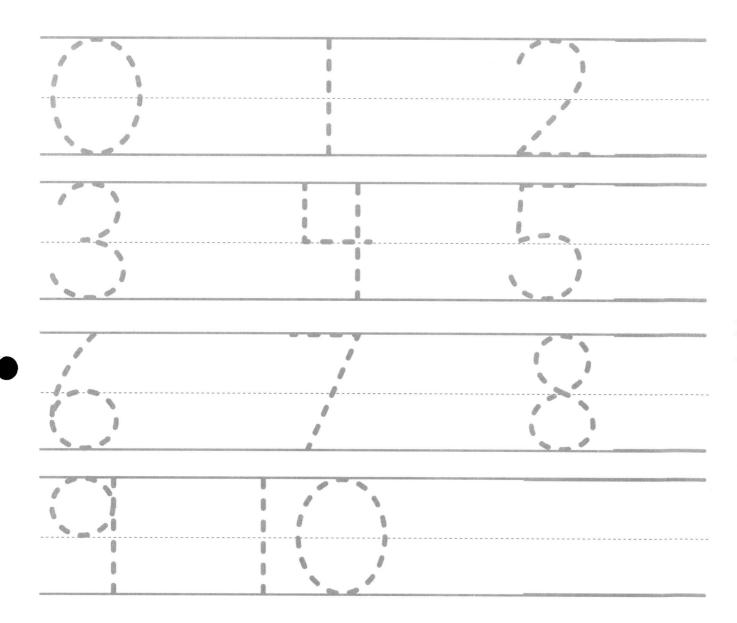

Remove from book and laminate. Use with washable markers.

Math Level K

Month _____

Sunday	Monday	Tuesday	Wednesday	Thursday	Friday	Saturday

JANUARY	JULY
FEBRUARY	AUGUST
MARCH	SEPTEMBER
APRIL	OCTOBER
MAY	NOVEMBER
JUNE	DECEMBER

Calendar Activities

Exercise 1

- Can you tell me what the month is on our Calendar?

- There are 7 days in a week, count to 7. Now, I want you to look at our Calendar.
  These 2 days are called the 'weekend'.

- The other 5 days are called weekdays.
  Let's point and count the weekdays.

Exercise 2

- Can you tell me what the month is on our Calendar?

- There are 7 days in a week, count to 7.
  Now, I want you to look at our Calendar.
  These 2 days are called the 'weekend'.

- The other 5 days are called weekdays.
  Let's point and count the weekdays.

Exercise 3

- There are 7 days in a week, count to 7.

- Remember, these 2 days are called the 'weekend'. The other 5 days are called weekdays. Let's point and count the weekdays.

- Can you tell me what two days of the week are the weekend?

Exercise 4

- There are 7 days in a week, count to 7.

- Point and count the weekdays.

Exercise 5

There are 7 days in a week, count to 7.

Point and count the weekdays.

Puzzle Solutions

Page 96

Page 298

Page 98

Page 304

Page 254

Page 337

Page 429

1	2	6	5
8	3	7	4

4	9	5	4	1	10
3	7	6	2	5	8
1	8	9	10		
5	4	2	3		